ΩΨΩΨΩΨΩΨΩΨΩΨΩΨΩΨΩΨΩΙ

C000185668

A DICTIONARY

OF

TRUANCY

by

Godfrey Holmes

ΩΨΩΨΩΨΩΨΩΨΩΨΩΨΩΨΩΨΩΨΩ

© **Godfrey Holmes**
Cover & all illustrations © Annamaria Dutto
September 2015

ISBN : 978-0-9536016-6-0

All rights reserved. No part of this publication may be reproduced
or transmitted in any form or by any means: electronic or
mechanical, including photocopying, recording - or entered into
any information storage and retrieval system -
nor may its content be incorporated
into staff training programmes,
without the prior permission, in writing, from the publisher.
A catalogue record of this Dictionary
is available from the British Library

NETHERMOOR BOOKS
"St. Elphin," 12 North Promenade,
Withernsea, East Riding , HU19 2DP

Telephone: 01964-615258
Contact the Author:
godfrey.holmes@btinternet.com

DEDICATED   TO
CHRIS   AND   JUDY -
WHO   LOOKED   OUT   FOR
THE   WANDERER

CONTENTS

....

ΩΨΩΨΩΨΩΨΩΨΩΨΩΨΩΨΩΨΩΨΩΨ

A DICTIONARY OF TRUANCY

••

INTRODUCTION

••

The birth of Truancy as "Social Problem" is also the birth of the State's obligation to provide schooling; each family's obligation to avail themselves of that education ; society evolving to the point it insists that children be educated less haphazardly than in Sunday Schools, Sabbath Schools, Poor Schools, Dame Schools, or Ragged Schools.

Most developed countries offer most parents the chance of some respite from parental responsibility - also new levels of attainment in reading and writing - in return for a promise that they will either send their child(ren) to some school, free at the point of use, or to some private school - nonsensically called a *Public* School - for which they must pay the whole or the part of any fee not covered by scholarship, bursary or endowment.

Truants are pupils who do not willingly take up the State's offer, nor avail themselves of any approved alternative. And, as is the way with all divergent or non-conformist behaviours, these absentee children are not aberrant *every single* day, neither for the whole of each day in question. Instead, they drift in and out of *deliberate* absence from school; in and out of absence from the classroom by default.

The word "*truant*" has a very interesting etymology. In the 13th. Century, the word derived from Old French for Beggar or Rogue: after an earlier Gaulish word : "*trougant.*" The Welsh language gave us the words : " *truan,*" or "*treuans*" for wretch, Gaelic giving us "*traughan*" for wretched. And drawing on the same source, the Spanish language provided us with "*truhan*" for a buffoon.

A truant with the specific meaning: "one who wanders from an appointed place," is used from the middle of the 15th. Century onward. In the literature of the 1540s. is also found truant as adjective : the truant(ing) subject, *playing* truant.

Here are one or two choice quotations relating to early truanting before the dominance of School Boards:

" *Yf the scholers were not beatedn and reprised of their truantrye, they shold neuer lerne*" 1481

" *Be Ye not ashamed the treuandes to play*" 1550

" Since I pluckt geese, plaide trewant and whipt top, I knew not what twas to be beaten....till lately" 1560

" A trewand knaue that faineth himself sicke when he shud woorke" 1561

" You, like wilful and truently children can neuer learne without whipping" 1579

" They may shune this sharpe schoolemaster by playing the trewans" 1642

" His troaning the schedule led to demotion to the lowest forme" 1690

" He gained his own education - though made of truantism, an incorrect one" 1812

" Infinite yawnings during lecture, and unquestionable gusto in the delights of truanting" 1887

Truants from the Board Schools first built under the Forster Act of 1870 are still labelled rogues (*trougants* roughing it?) or, less commonly, folk-heroes. That we need folk heroes is evidenced in the fascination - adulation? - popular culture, puzzlingly, illogically, devotes to the Great Train Robbers, the Kray Twins, also those criminals digging deep in order to open safety deposit boxes.

The case *against* the truant, indeed against the temptation and fulfilment of Truancy itself, is almost unanswerable: unanswerable in the eyes, and according to the remit, of the educational and political establishment; also beyond contradiction among the so-called commentariat. As always, media maketh the man.

Perhaps self-evidently, the truant is surely a *disruptive* force : disrupting the ebb and flow of life and of school life - away when he should be there; requiring to be chased up when his peers do not need chasing up; missing some vital Lessons; unable to keep up with whatever the class is doing upon a truant's return.

Furthermore, surely the truant must be *up to no good* while not seated where they should be : behind a desk. Is (s)he causing mayhem in the rose garden of his local park? Perhaps (s)he is clearing the shelves of an edge-of-town Tesco Superstore ? Or maybe (s)he is sniffing glue, snorting cocaine, out of a bread bag past its sell-by date? Perhaps truants make ideal look-outs, runners, or foils, for someone with far more evil intent than themselves?

And what of the *female* truant's welfare, girls in focus, while she is out of the classroom? Is she hungry? Is she pregnant? Is she prey to exploitative couriers, taxi-drivers, or sellers of hot-dogs? Maybe she is being used as household skivvy, cheap babysitter: surrounded by dirty pots, wet sheets and screaming toddlers? Unhappy: unhappily; at risk: unarguably.

But there *is* another, and different, perspective on the phenomenon of Truancy: welcoming truants, welcoming their non-conformism, and welcoming them back. An unexpected perspective this; unconventional; inconvenient. Folk devil truants to whom ? Folk *hero* truants to whom ? And could this, more charitable, more nuanced, view of truants ever win hearts and minds?

From this angle, the truant is only doing what wider society normally would ask him to do in a post-Thatcher era: *exercise choice.* Choice of GP: good. Choice of hospital: good. Choice of gas supplier: good. Choice of ISA: good. Choice of grocer: good. Choice of secondary school: good. *Choice of whether to attend that high school :* bad ?

Very few Social Services are compulsory - beyond some admissions to psychiatric hospitals, all admissions to prison; and the mass immunization, and birth registration, of new infants come to mind as relying for their reach on the diminution of choice. But people are not routinely *forced* to visit the dentist, or apply for State Pension, or accept a home help across one's doorstep, or take up *Motability*. Darby and Joan Clubs are optional in old age - as is U3A membership or the fitting of a stair-lift.

Yet accessing education is *compulsory*. Ironically, should any pupil insist on opting out, that child would be informing service-providers where they might do their jobs much better - much as filling in Trip Advisor for a restaurant or hotel stay can instantly improve that establishment's attraction and profitability.

Also worth noting : opting out need not be opting out *forever*. A transient truant might return to informal education at WEA, or in the local library, or Open University, or seated in front of BBC 4 TV. Truants must access some learning just by being out and about. Proof of this universal, unbounded, input comes with enterprising Home Educators who offer their children solely a Nature Studies' / Great Outdoors' / Architectural Appreciation / Museum Visit / watch-and-see programme of study.

However, the *strongest* defence of Truancy is probably the benefit that the scholar *not at school* brings to his or her own family and the wider economy.

Some children who face difficulty attending school spend those "hours of freedom" caring for younger siblings: thus saving everyone nursery fees. Other children, it can be argued, are essential for the day-to-day, hour-by-hour, care of parents and grandparents, also siblings, suffering great disability: such restricted movement - on the part of both carer and cared for - that Nursing Home might be the only realistic alternative.

Yet other children truant in order to enhance the family income, to boost the domestic economy, or at least not depleting it, as might be the case with all the extra expense of bus-fares, uniform, books, dinner money. There might be precious little food, no dry bedding, no comfortable furniture, in the home. Mum might be an *Avon* or *Bettaware* Rep. Or Dad might be downstairs serving ale 84 hours a week, so needing someone to do the books and clean the glasses. The whole family might be on the move with the circus, or as scrap metal merchants: so needing someone, literally, to keep the caravan or fairground ride on the road.

Local authorities and schools alike tend to stress the "Escape from" angle of the Truancy debate, not the "Escape to." Therefore the economic benefits of an extra person out on the field, the tulip field, the turnip field, is underestimated - unless the absentee from the classroom happens to be a strapping 17-year old father or a more-than-capable 15-year old mother.

Finally, still in defence of Truancy: although the truant, or suspected truant, is called "disruptive," many absentees actually *reduce* disruption in class by being away from the fray. 27 pupils are generally easier to teach than 31. And the teacher who has to stop every few minutes to calm down a borderline-hyperactive child already *rejoices at* the fixed-term suspension, or total expulsion, of that child. So why not adopt that same sense of relief when unauthorized absentees are absent - without having to resort to suspension?

****

In order to compile this Dictionary, I have needed to create a whole matrix of dots on a page and then attempt to join them up.. Discussion of *Academies* has led to *Arms-Length* Governance. Student *Poverty* has inevitably resulted in attention to student *Hunger*. Meanwhile, *Boredom* has been accepted as a contributor to Truancy, not just in its own right, but as correlative to *Hyperactivity*. Going even further, the possibility of *Hyperactivity* has incontestably led to consideration of *Parenting* / and *Parenting Classes*.

Such joining up of those dots tantalizingly results in omission. *Some* omissions happen in avoidance of the banal; at other times, to rise above vain repetition; elsewhere, to preclude stating the obvious; whilst yet more omissions are completely unintentional: the sort that might be remedied in future editions of this Dictionary, when readers say: "Did you ever think of *that* attribute? / that scare? / that problem? / that solution/ that inconvenience ?

Many are the *straight* analyses of the phenomenon of Truancy: written chapter by chapter. In the format of a Dictionary I take a completely different route : the alphabetical exploration of all, or nearly all, the divergent forces that mysteriously converge within and without *one specific behaviour*; because the Author maintains that some of these forces - very exciting and intriguing forces - would be lost in lengthy prose.

The Author wishes teachers and parents and education administrators alike to think outside the box ; to wander on to everybody else's territory ; to link up their hitherto disjointed trains of thought; and to treat the truant himself, the truant herself, as *real people,* fully sentient subjects : *interesting* people who come to life when they shorn of cheap and demeaning labels; caring people who have chosen to put on the garments of responsible citizenship, albeit rather unconventional citizenship.

In summary, if schools and society are *certain* of the quality and quantity of what young people are offered either within their walls or on the campus of the local Tech, children will be queueing up for that input on September 1st., even though Term may not start until September 3rd. ; and,   crucially, those sometimes troubled young people will feel able to acquaint their Heads of Year with the pressures they are under; the competing demands made on their daytime hours; childhoods curtailed due to adult responsibilities; interrupted night-times;   all the stresses that, unforeseen, have accumulated within their *blended* households, without subterfuge, *without Truancy.*

G.H.H.
Withernsea
June 2015

A NOTE ABOUT LAYOUT

....

Each entry below is given a score of 1 to 10. That score relates <u>only</u> to the importance of that contributing factor or obstacle or response to the whole Truancy Debate. So a score of 6 when discussing Truancy might score 10 in a study of Fostering. Similarly a score of 9 - and I have needed to award more 9s and 10s than I could ever have anticipated - in a Dictionary of Truancy might be reduced to 2 in a Hobby Manual.

Capitals are employed fairly freely. That usage arises partly from the specialness of what is under discussion : eg. Crown Court, Prime Minister, Government, Adolescent Unit. Then the actual word Truancy is acknowledged as central to everything by award of a capital. Further, Truancy would be left too exposed if necessary qualifications, such as suspected / attempted / habitual Truancy do not sometimes carry a Capital also. The verbs: "truanting" and "playing truant" are necessarily lower-case.

Where there are two or more possible titles for a particular entry: eg. Tracking <u>or</u> GPS, the more commonly-used word(s) come first; the alternative, in brackets, second. Very occasionally, the alternative deserves an entry all of its own.

Then, to rid the text of "Please see"s and "cf"s, a diamond symbol : ◇ is inserted wherever the reader would benefit from turning to an associated entry earlier or later in the Dictionary. Almost every significant entry in the Dictionary does in fact carry a ◇ - because Truancy is such a complex phenomenon, it reaches the parts simpler behaviours do not.

ΩΨΩΨΩΨΩΨΩΨΩΨΩΨΩ

AN A - Z OF TRUANCY

••

ACADEMIES....6

Academies - also Free Schools - impact upon Truancy in two distinct ways. First, the original Academies and City Technology Colleges◊ were such attractive places to learn that disaffected teenagers almost clamoured to enrol: somewhere different to learn, subjects more practical, greater capitation allowances.

Second, and now that Academies / Free Schools are more widespread, less of a novelty, not ever so distinguishable from their local Comps, their very existence makes the intending truant less detectable. truants have the explanation of longer, more complex, cross-city journeys to reach their Academies ; different uniform◊ ; later hours; divergent half-term holidays◊ ; alternative outside assignments to complete : all means of fobbing off anybody who questions them as to why they are not being educated where the people stopping them in the street assume they are being educated. In fact, truants would lose their street-credibility◊ if they *didn't* fall between every stool.

[THE] ACCEPTABLE BEHAVIOUR
CONTRACT 6

The Acceptable Behaviour Contract has been employed at least 20000 times in the United Kingdom as an earlier intervention than the ASBO◇. For truants, this essentially non-enforceable document is drawn up between the school, suspected truant, and that truant's parent or guardian. Such a Contract can be very wide-ranging, dealing with dress, attitude, school rules or behaviour in class - as well as Truancy. Nor does such a Contract have to be referred to Police or to a Youth Court ◇. In one form or another it has actually been around as long as "Contract Theory" in Social Psychology ◇: that perfect analogy between commercial contracts signed and sealed, and good intention contracts ready to be signed and sealed.

AIDING AND ABETTING....7

The Aiding and Abetting test - or accusation - is brought into play where an Attendance Officer◇ has suspicion a parent or responsible adult is colluding◇ with the child / "patient," in order to evade School. Common charges are that parent-figures have not been *curious* enough; that they did not set the alarm clock early enough ; that they did not mend the torn trousers soon enough ; that they did not accompany their child to the school gate ; that they used a child for the personal care of themselves◇ or the prosperity of the family business.. all in school time.

Of interest, Aiding and Abetting is the presumption until anybody proves otherwise. So the charge is very difficult for a parent to argue against : " Nothing anyone can do!" " You know what she's like..." " Got a mind of his own!" "We've tried everything!" It takes a bold, and skilled, magistrate to determine who exactly is telling the truth, and which first-timer in Court◇ deserves the benefit of the doubt.

ALCOHOL / CONSUMING ALCOHOL....8

Just as there is an enormous correlation between smoking◇ and Truancy, so is there a known and quantifiable relationship between Alcohol Consumption and bunking off◇. Also, smoking and the habitual drinking of alcohol are themselves linked to each other- as one doctor put it: "like Beyonce and sold-out concerts."

The child / teenager drinking under-age (up to a fifth of 13 year-olds, a third of 15 year-olds, half of all 6th-formers, drinking regularly) is laying up trouble for the future. Whoever says drinking will diminish after flying back from holiday / after the next match / after exams◇, whatever, is living in fantasy-land.

While no parent, teacher or commentator should worry about occasional dabbling, curious experimentation, or a glass of wine at a family celebration: pre-tanking, binge-drinking, secret drinking sessions, after-breakfast drinking, are all cause for concern.

Collusion must definitely not be ruled out here. 100 Parents were offered a fridge / larder padlock, so that their children might not illicitly access Alcohol stored in the home. Yet only 2% of those 100 subjects took up the offer. Other times, a parent does not notice / admonish their intoxicated child; nor ask where (s)he has been, and with whom ; nor confiscate both the alcohol and the money to buy that alcohol. Not for nothing is alcohol labelled: "Legalized Drug Addiction."◇ - though the two are not exact equivalents, by any measure.

So what advantage has the truanting drinker got above a presentee◇ companion? First Truancy allows speedier and longer access to sources of alcohol : the empty apartment , cave, a friend's fridge, local superstore (nicked), Sugar Daddy. Sugar Daddies have been prominent in the news from 2005 forwards for their enterprising - and wicked - skills tempting young women, in particular, with cigarettes, cash, bottles of plonk, jewellery and drugs, in return for sexual favours and rape. Working together.

Truancy also provides a suitable *occasion* to drink, alone - or, still better, in the company of mates. Not only that: Truancy allows the time and space for recovery from a bad hangover; from a party that was certainly fuelled; from the disco that lasted to the early hours. Nor should we forget how underage drinking is both risky◇ and exciting, just as Truancy is risky and exciting. Cheap thrills

ALIBIS....8

An Alibi for Truancy is not quite the same as *an excuse*◇ or an explanation. A good Alibi depends on a reliable witness : eg a parent who has seen their child at the bedside of an iller child◇; a librarian who vouches seeing the suspected truant in Local History; an usher who was showing another witness into Youth Court◇. Even so, some people are ready to give a false Alibi to rescue a friend / acquaintance from punishment◇ / wrath.

Naturally, not a few head teachers doubt the authenticity of Alibis - especially if the suspect has past form. And every single Alibi cannot be looked into. It is then the benefit of the doubt comes into play. Also a sensitive head has nothing to gain from rejecting, instantly, every Alibi, every excuse. The child's *trust* must be won back - because all school attendance is ultimately all about trust◇ and reward◇.

ALIENATION....8

Alienation in relation to Truancy has two distinct meanings. One sense is "literally" to become an Alien. And that is a useful metaphor because, unless the truant arrived on a plane from Timbuktu yesterday, (s)he is not Alien foreigner - rather Alien *feeling like* foreigner in his own homestead or school classroom or neighbourhood. Once made an Alien - either through bullying or stereotyping - there is no reason for Alien truant to attend school more than ritually.

A second meaning, far more common, reveals itself when the truant gradually *distances* himself/herself from their surroundings : from bewilderment, *mis-fitting*◇, *non-conformism*◇, anomie, imagining oneself to be the outsider◇, *semi-detachment*. That latter expression, taken from architecture, is especially useful. For it describes somebody half in and half out ; not sure where or when to show his hand of cards. It also incorporates the concept of Mental Truancy◇.

ALTERNATIVE DISPUTE RESOLUTION....7

Rather than rushing to Youth Court◇, other courts, fines◇ or retribution, following discovered, uncovered, Truancy, far better that a head teacher, in conjunction with aggrieved parents, goes for Alternative Dispute Resolution. Governors or the local authority can easily set this Resolution in train, aided by the good offices of an independent mediator.

The great advantage of sitting round a table, in a collegiate atmosphere, is the avoidance or mitigation of future confrontation◇. And because Dispute Resolution, without resort to prosecution, leaves everyone feeling better - later, harsher, options might be negated. The disaffected teenager might even find here a welcome forum for speaking up for himself/herself. Nor does anybody loses face or faith. Indeed, everybody wishes to get matters to right for the future.

AMPLIFICATION....8

Amplification is the sociological term for the escalation that makes an uncomplicated situation much bigger - or worse - by enlarging its impact ; blowing it out of all proportion. Typically a teenager shouts at a lifeguard who then calls in the leisure manager who then calls in the Police who then asks for back-up...and so on.

When isolated - or easily explainable - instances of Truancy come to light, the emphasis should be on de-escalation: the opposite of Amplification. That is because, if a heavy-end response becomes the *first* response, no option is left for later on. A word in a form-tutor's ear, or a no-panic text to a parent, might be quite sufficient to begin with. After all, teenagers will face a lot more perils in their school-lives other than a Friday afternoon watching Wimbledon semi-finals.

ANTI-SOCIAL HABITS....6

Most school children are fun to be with: lively, amusing, engaging. Just a few children, however, have Anti-Social Habits which make them rather hard to like: spitting, nasal care, flashing, head-banging, chewing cloth. Worse, if the child concerned suffers learning difficulty◊, such Habits might be *ignored*, even excused. Better perhaps that Anti-Social Habits are addressed first off. Still, their very existence provides a possible prompt for Truancy - as most school pupils are surprisingly cute when it comes to judging which behaviours will be tolerated or not tolerated.

APARTHEID....6

Apartheid is alive and well in education. The potential truant might not only find himself or herself in a Church of England School rather than its Catholic equivalent ; the child tempted to bunk off might be one of the indigenous minority in a predominantly ethnic School; more commonly, a black child in an outer-urban or country school opening its doors to mostly "White British" admissions. A third, and influential, aspect of Apartheid is the way most school catchment areas are organized according to post code, rather than across defined geographical entities. This latter pattern of separate existence can also lead to the nurture of gangs◇. And as in so many fields, stereotyping◇ is more easily accomplished where there is hatred and suspicion based on faith or the ghetto.

APPRENTICESHIPS.....4

Until Alan, Lord Sugar, and later Tony Blair, stepped into the breach, the very word "Apprenticeship" faced extinction: a rite of passage more suited to 1910 than 2010. However, successive Governments intent on massaging high unemployment statistics and "keeping kids off the street" have enthusiastically embraced the notion, if not the authentic ritual, of Apprenticeship.

So why not allow all potential truants the chance to begin their Apprenticeships at aged 15? Therewith they would see the immediate application of all the skills and mathematics they have learnt or would hope to have learnt by then. Apprentices also deserve higher pay.

APPROVED SCHOOL....5

Historically, and of interest, right up until the early 1980s, truants could be sent to Approved Schools - where sometimes they also truanted from the lessons laid on in the Approved School education wing ! Approved Schools were sometimes called Schools of Correction, Children's Centres, or Residential Children's Units, but an important plank of social policy at the time was a firm belief that Truancy was perfectly sufficient reason to send a child away from his or her own home; whereas a more modern approach is to offer community support for the truant and his/her birth family / extended family, actually in the home.

One extra side-effect of sending a simple truant to Approved School is the possibility of amplification◊ whereby they would, most likely, meet therein young people "in Care" far worse than themselves : hardened offenders, drug addicts, glue-sniffers, self-harmers, vandals. So, keeping these school dodgers closest to chance of turn-around and redemption makes sense.

[THE] ARMED FORCES....5

The Armed Forces in England and Wales are ready to take Cadets on their 16th. birthdays - and put them into battle at 17. So it is that the Armed Forces have become the traditional refuge for sometimes bored◊ or disillusioned young people wanting a life of excitement, some independence, order, the chance to travel, and a uniform.

Truants may be far less eager to miss school if the Army Recruitment Sergeant is going to ask about attendance; about past trouble in or out of the classroom; or about overall appearance and attitude. In other words, the Army acts as incentive: incentive to see schooling out, incentive to be the best. The Army can take under its wings those lads - also a few girls - who might not have made the grade in a local vocational apprenticeship◊ or in Further Education◊. At the other end of the spectrum, the Armed Forces are very proud bodies fishing in the same pool as sixth-form colleges / universities for the brightest, most highly-attaining recruits; for pupils of Officer calibre.

ARSON....4

Satan finds a work for idle hands to do: so the proverb goes. Arson is a terrible crime: so awful that it is often downgraded to criminal damage by Police who dare not speak its name. And there are particular *seats* of Arson: letter-boxes, rubbish bins, parched forests, deserted factories and warehouses, churches and chapels.

Fire-raising to or within religious buildings arguably amounts to sacrilege - but even that word is rarely used. Yet churches - like stately homes - are far more likely to be torched than buildings less iconic. And that fire damage takes years, decades, to repair.

There has to be some overlap between Truancy and Arson: not that truants are inherently malign, but because Arson in remote areas, or remote alcoves of abandoned buildings much nearer home, needs some planning, also fewer potential child witnesses / grasses, than regular school hours allow.

ASBOs
[ANTI-SOCIAL BEHAVIOUR ORDERS]....6

The British government introduced ASBOs within the Crime and Disorder Act 1998. In the UK, a CRASBO is a "criminally related" ASBO. One local authority has published photos of those awarded ASBOs on an Internet site. Anti-social behaviour includes this range of problems:

- abandoning cars
- arson◇
- begging
- the caste system
- dangerous driving
- defecating / urinating in public
- disturbing the peace
- dogging (exhibitionistic public sex)
- drug dealing / consumption of controlled recreational drugs◇
- drunken behaviour◇
- fare evasion
- homophobia◇
- intimidation◇
- littering / fly tipping / dog fouling
- loitering (with intent)
- noise pollution
- paedophilic activity
- racism◇
- rioting
- rudeness◇
- smoking in public places◇
- spitting / stealing / mugging / shoplifting◇
- urban exploration - also vandalism / criminal damage ◇ / graffiti.

Although more associated with juvenile delinquents, ASBOs are a useful civil or civic remedy for adult misbehaviour too. Thus it is possible that the truant will have earned his ASBO for non-school based misdemeanours; his Dad for all these, but also for permitting, colluding with◇, his children's Truancy.

To obtain an ASBO, a two-stage test must be satisfied by the applicant authority (see Sn..1(1) of the Crime and Disorder Act 1998). The first is that the defendant has committed acts causing, or likely to cause, harassment, alarm or distress within six months of the date of issue of the summons. The second is that an order is necessary to protect persons from further anti-social behaviour◇.

For England and Wales, the Antisocial Behaviour, Crime and Policing Act, given royal assent in March 2014, replaces the previously controversial ASBOs with civil injunctions and new Criminal Behaviour Orders. The crime then lies in ignoring any foregoing injunction, not in the imposition of the CBO itself.

ATTENDING FOR REGISTRATION ONLY....8

As old as the Attendance Register is the practice / device of Attending for Registration Only - then bunking off◇. This is often easier said than done: due to lesson swipe-cards◇, sentinels, and security fences◇. On the other hand, the truant is far less likely to face detection if (s)he is centrally registered, registered online, or registered by an ally, only at the very start of the day or start of afternoon session.

ANTI-TRUANCY DRIVES....8

Anti-Truancy Drives / Anti-Truancy Campaigns, are extremely important and influential. With these offensives, all the relevant agencies tighten up on Truancy, at exactly the same time; intensifying their efforts to get errant children back into the classroom. The only trouble is: you cannot keep up an Anti-Truancy Drive forever. The novelty wears off, as schools get back to normal.

ANTI-TRUANCY SWEEPS....8

A Truancy Sweep is a little different from a Truancy Drive◇. A Sweep is very *unlikely* to be announced. Instead, Police, teachers, and welfare officers◇ descend on to a seafront, steaming any amusement arcade or popular shopping mall. Within the orbit of the Sweep, every child of school attendance age is questioned as to the credentials of their absence; then returned home, or to their places of learning, according to whatever protocol is in place.

ANXIETY....8

All truants are Anxious - if only to avoid detection and punishment. However, the Anxiety most truants experience is a state of mind: bewilderment, siege, wariness, torment◊, heightened awareness - all these ingredients of a panic attack. So when a truant is caught, and later recalled to school, his head of year should bear Anxiety in mind: Anxiety as a cluster of fears◊, not one single mind-set.

ARMS-LENGTH EDUCATION....4

Arms Length Education happens whenever a school or local authority delegates the duty of teaching and learning to a different person or institution: whether to the teacher as also parent of a child, private tutor, remedial tutor◊, academy◊, or college of further education◊. In these instances, some young people are bound to fall between the cracks; or else they have a ready-made alibi◊: that they were already on their way to somewhere else, like the dentist or the sports' hall, where they ought to be just now.

ARREST FOR SOMETHING DIFFERENT....5

When an adolescent is stopped or arrested by Police for Something Completely Different from Truancy: shoplifting◇, possession of an illegal substance◇, dangerous cycling, begging, loitering with intent, ABH, criminal damage◇, whatever, they or Social Services might also discover (s)he is truanting from school. And, although that discovery is *accidental,* it is sufficient to bring the absenteeism that might until then have been "explained," or overlooked, back into the frame....surely a hornet's nest.

Arrest is far more likely on school days because truanting scholars are more visible - with almost everyone else of that age seated in the classroom. Store detectives are particularly alert to Truancy financed by, or hiding behind, shop theft. So when ignominy comes, the shame is doubled. Parents are called to attend the Police Station not for one thing but two.

ATTENDANCE AT SCHOOL FORBIDDEN....7

The State concedes that some children are forbidden to Attend School on account of past misdemeanours, migration status, or their family's reluctance to apologize for whatever led to exclusion◇ / expulsion◇. What puzzles the State is when aggrieved, overburdened, parents also forbid the School Attendance that could, potentially, relieve them of many of their anxieties, whilst also ensuring their children are fed.

They might so do because of their faith◊, their dissatisfaction with sex education, their hatred of Western literature, a past grudge, resentment that their child(ren) did not get their first choice of School◊ - or worry that the domestic economy◊ will collapse in the absence of one of the only two identifiable breadwinners.

ATTENDANCE ORDERS....9

Any option or punishment available to a court is called a "disposal." In other words, these endings ensure *throughput* within our courts - whilst also providing some sense of closure. *Attendance Orders* are a very valued disposal: partly because they are so specific.

Through the Attendance Order, the court places the responsibility firmly on the shoulders of a parent or parent-figure to get a child to the actual school gate. And the beauty of the Attendance Order is that it is incontrovertible, not easily misinterpreted. If a parent is *ordered* to facilitate a far greater number of half-days' Attendance until the court re-convenes, (s)he cannot grumble about the suddenness - and unfairness - of any consequent prosecution. Naturally, Attendance Orders do not have to be for *100%* attendance; nor force a genuinely ill child to rise from his or her sick-bed; merely for significant and measurable *improvement* in attendance patterns, however responsible / keen / or irresponsible the actual child happens to be.

ATTENTION DEFICIT HYPERACTIVITY DISORDER....5

There is irreconcilable debate among experts surrounding ADHD and "an answer" to ADHD: whether it should be drug therapy ? Or should it be behaviour therapy? Should it perhaps be some rebalancing of a child's diet? Or should it be plain and simple punishment◇? Solution is greatly hampered by no common agreement as to whether this syndrome *actually exists*? Sceptics are certain ADHD is a posh-sounding, sanitized, creation to cover (or cover-up?) plain *naughtiness.*

However, there are enough educational psychologists, enough parents, enough GPs, who *do* subscribe to ADHD - and its Turrets' variation - to keep schools and Youth Courts◇ alert as to that post-War syndrome's destructive - and unattractive - repercussions. And one thing is certain: *if* ADHD is a myth, a similar configuration of antisocial behaviours◊ would have to be invented.

Taking all that taken into account, some parents, many teachers, and not a few perplexed police officers, fiercely oppose the medicalization of the overactive children in their charge. They do not want Ritalin. Nor Largactil : the liquid cosh. Nor sedatives. Nor Prozac. Nor anti-depressants. Nor an Adolescent Unit attached to the Infirmary. Instead: Cognitive Behavioural Therapy, other "talking therapies," anger-management, solution-focused counselling, star charts, triggered rewards: all these are much preferred.

Do children with ADHD also truant? The correlation is much clearer the milder the Attention Deficit. That is because full-blown ADHD would be too aggravating, too awkward, too cataclysmic, to hide from curious shopkeepers, pedestrians or onlookers. Truants need to keep below the parapet; and ADHD doesn't exactly achieve that.

AVERSION TO ALL TEACHERS....6
Improbable it is that one child could develop an Aversion to All Teachers, but it does happen where school and home have a long history of clashes and

distrust◇; also where the home relies on stereotypes◇ applying to *all* teachers / all Police / all Social Workers/ all housing officers / all health visitors....all "scum." The hostile child has only the hostility that surrounds them in the home or the run-down neighbourhood to imbibe and to feast on.

AVERSION TO ALL AUTHORITY....8

"Authority" is difficult to describe - but we certainly know what it is it when we're up against it. Authority is a gargantuan monolith: a dreadful spectre, harder and harsher, more impossible to reason with, than any other immoveable force. Truants, generally, have an Aversion to Authority; their parents, maybe a learnt Aversion to All Authority.

AVERSION TO ONE TEACHER....7

Should there be a clash of school child and school teacher where that one teacher - maybe a form teacher ? remedial teacher ? primary school class teacher ? - is the one the wobbly child *sees most of*, the temptation will exist to truant in order to get away from the grip of that one person. The same could well happen with Aversion to just *One Head Teacher* where parent-figures imagine that leader "has it in for" Avril or Augustus, Wendy or William.

AWOL : "Absence WithOut Leave"....by definition. See Bunking off

BABYSITTING....6

Unusual among household tasks, Babysitting can be handsomely rewarded: especially when that Babysitting is for a neighbour / relative / friend of parent, rather than for a toddler within the absentee's / presentee's own home. More labelled◇ truants than usually accounted for are dragged into (largely unpaid) Babysitting for siblings and step-siblings they have perhaps resented as new additions to their families in the first place; imposters who demand that bigger slice of family income, family food fare.

To the outside world, school-day Babysitting is marked down, or flagged up, as Truancy - which it isn't, at least not in the accepted sense. Therefore it is incumbent on form tutors and Head Teachers to ask about Babysitting obligations first and foremost.

Everybody needs to understand that there are a few households which will not survive without the ministry of plenteous teenaged Babysitters, often unrewarded, stepping into the breach not least during a toddler's illness. Mum herself might be at the Surgery with yet another ill sibling whilst the teenager holds the fort for the remainder. Or Dad might have to pop to the Job Centre, then bring home some bread and marmalade.

BAGGAGE....8

In Psychology, "Baggage" means the luggage everyone carries round with them in their dealings and in their relationships. Sometimes this Baggage is so heavy that no new partner or associate can lift it, or relieve its burden. It just gets dumped wherever it is allowed to be dumped.

Pupils who truant, almost by definition, are carrying Baggage round with them. Perhaps School, family too, overlooked this impediment before family breakdown; before the crisis or crunch-point came along; before the great escape. Some students actually *need* a few hours on their own to shed a little Baggage.

[YOU WOULD BE] BETTER OFF WITHOUT ME ! 5

All children, at one time or another in their upbringing, say : "You'd Be Better Off Without Me !" This throwaway (?) comment, this lament, could be directed at a sibling playing a game rather too single-mindedly; the child who gets that other child into trouble; the child who blames the other child for "ruining everything";

the mother, nerves shredded, preparing the family picnic ; the whole family wanting to watch Britain's Got Talent without interruption; companion at a particularly stand-offish disco - or class teacher.

"You'd Be Better Off Without Me!" is calculated blackmail; also notice of imminent withdrawal. It is a statement far more directed at those who *stay* than those who turn away. Suicide is the ultimate manifestation of: "You'd Be Better Off Without Me!": a comment not upon death but on life and the living people remaining; remaining full of guilt and regret that they did not do enough to rescue their loved one on board. Truants, though thankfully *not* usually suicidal, opt out because it causes them fewer problems than opting in. Additionally, they have frequently heard all-or-nothing statements coming out of their harassed parents' mouths.

BOREDOM....9

The subject of Boredom is amazingly difficult to address - because it means something different to every single human being: a variation of what is sometimes called: "the Boredom Threshold." To such an extent that not a few psychologists dismiss or distrust the notion of Boredom altogether. And call it lethargy or inertia.

If Boredom *does* exist and *does* spread its wings and fly into the lives of people old and young, employed or unemployed, child-burdened as well as child-free, single as well as married: then it will impact upon truants, and tempted truants, too.

Truants might even give "Boredom" as their central reason for Truancy : triple boredom. Because, first, thousands of disaffected teenagers are bored in the classroom, bored stiff. They have to lend their ears and attention for 35, 45 or 70 minutes at a stretch - and it *is* a stretch for them. Then they have to do coursework, homework and computer-work, as well as listen to teachers going on and on and on. Only crafts, domestic science and sport provides some relief (release ?) from Boredom in the classroom.

Second, most truants are bored *at home* : bored stiff. Bored downstairs ; bored upstairs . Bored waiting to be fed; bored eating the boring food when it arrives. Bored in front of the telly ; bored playing Scrabble; bored tending to the wants of elderly grandparents, the wants too of their own or disabled *parents* ; bored looking after younger siblings; bored on Saturday ; bored on Sunday.

Third, most truants are bored whilst actually truanting. That sounds like a contradiction. However, much Truancy is the spending of hours and hours in a cave or bus shelter ; hours and hours on a park or promenade bench ; hours and hours in the loft, evading capture ; hours and hours extra in bed, pretending to be iller than one really is.

Therefore, *any* response to Truancy must also be a response to Boredom. And that entails *a societal* response to Poverty - because poor children are far more susceptible to Boredom than middle- or upper-class children with few if any money worries. And school lessons must be made more engaging, more exciting : more daring ; more interactive : not every lesson - but enough lessons to draw the wanderer in, if only for P.E. and footie next.

BORN IN AUGUST....5

English and Welsh schools have traditionally made 12-01am, September 1st., the dividing line between a child being placed in one year at school or the next intake. So it is that the July- or August-born pupil enters school - and leaves school - a few months earlier than their September-born neighbours and contemporaries.

Perhaps unwittingly, some commentators, some teachers, respond by *pitying*, rather than envying, the child born so soon before September 1st. for always being youngest ; therefore less exposed to reading and writing; less equipped to battle it out in the classroom with boys and girls who may be up to 10 months older than they.

BORN IN SEPTEMBER
[OR EARLY OCTOBER]....7

Scholars born after 12-01am, September 1st., are frequently angry and frustrated that they will probably stay a whole year extra behind their desks, longer than a child down the road born on August 23rd or 31st. And to make matters worse, there is a significant spike in births between September 10th and 30th. There did used to be *Easter* leaving-dates for children caught up in the September trap. No longer. So perhaps September/ October birth is an inducement to Truancy / getting a paid job as early as not possible.

BREADWINNERS....8

Many children old before their time have "to volunteer" to become a family's Breadwinner. Especially where one or both parents have died or have flitted ; or where one parent is severely disabled ; or where money is so short within a household that a few pounds, cash-in-hand, is the difference between sinking and swimming. Schoolchild Breadwinners act as babysitters◊, home-workers◊, couriers, bookies' runners, druggie-runners◊, cleaners, vegetable gatherers, vegetable preparers - or else they work in back-street factories for minimal reward.

Yet to be family Breadwinner is also an honour and satisfaction. Some parents - not a few - collude◊ with their children's presence in field or warehouse because the money is so vital; the chance of discovery relatively remote, due to a weak and depleted and overstretched inspectorate. Then there might be extra treats, smart-phones and rewards for the youngest Breadwinner in the household : a type of reward for enterprise.

Naturally, local authorities have no truck with young earners◊, unless their hours are very few, licensed, and unlikely to interfere with schoolwork. Occasionally, illegal young employees are flushed out of shed or garage or sweatshop: slightly more difficult an operation when all the breadwinning is done in, or from, the Schoolchild Breadwinner's own home.

BUNKING OFF....by definition

All behaviours attract alternative descriptions : *pork pies* for lies, *making off with* for theft, *joy-riding* for vehicle-taking, *getting copped* for apprehending. With Truancy, children use the actual word "Truancy" relatively infrequently. "Skiving" sounds better; and doubtless there are numerous nationwide and regional synonyms : skipping◊, ditching, playing hookey (or hookie), mitching, playing marikar, throwing a sickie, slacking, wagging◊ (wagging off), punching, suffering acute skivitis, AWOL◊ (going AWOL ; formally : Absent Without Leave - an Armed Forces'◊ term) or RHINO◊ (formally : Rarely Here, Name Only, or Here in Name Only ; actually makes little sense in its fullest form : Rarely Here In Name Only - unless, of course, a comma appears : Rarely Here, Name Only).

BULLYING....10

The subject of Bullying is far too big for a Dictionary - except a Dictionary of Bullying! - deserving a book, or a library, of its own. Nevertheless, Bullying impacts upon Truancy so greatly that it has to be given due coverage.

Does Bullying start with Parenthood◇ or Siblinghood? Or is it even older : ingrained in human nature before birth or subsequent nurture ? Is Bullying, perhaps, a complex *learnt* behaviour? And, if so, is it imitative, or responsive to "go and do likewise"? Moreover, is Bullying a conscious, doled out, behaviour or an experienced behaviour - or both ?

What is certain is that Bullying leads to both Truancy and Attempted Truancy; to self-harm◇ and attempted self-harm; at worst, to suicide◇ and attempted suicide. So great are the pressures of Bullying on teenagers - who then often go home to see one of their parents being bullied - that Truancy is almost automatic in the circumstances. Indeed, Truancy as reasoned response to Bullying, sometimes has to be dressed up as illness; or else its direct consequence is very real *Mental Illness*◇.

And in our understanding of - or failure to understand - the phenomenon of Bullying, there swiftly arrives one of its stable-mates : Bully himself being bullied; fear◇ of the Bully; pity for the Bully; extended Bullying; denied Bullying; undisclosed Bullying; condoned Bullying...the list is long, even not taking into account Cyber-Bullying◇ and the so-called Cycle of Bullying.

Many a child tells a father-figure, mother or teacher that (s)he is being Bullied - whereupon (s)he is told (s)he must put up with it, ignore it, escape it, report it higher, confront it, forget it. Some of these automatic adult responses to Bullying are hopelessly inadequate and insensitive to the extent that Bullies are allowed to prosper - and continue their Bullying - while the victim/ survivor is blamed for being thin-skinned ; blamed for crying ; blamed for telling tales ; blamed for *Truanting*.

Everyone be assured : if Bullying is not assessed and faced up to, each and every time, with zero-tolerance, Truancy, self-harm◇, Mental Illness◇, copied Bullying, and suicide◇, will rocket.

BURYING THEIR HEADS IN THE SAND....6

Yes, parents do sometimes Bury their Heads in the Sand. After all, they are closest to most suspected truants. They understand their offspring; understand, literally, where their children and stepchildren are coming from. So, should they do [foolishly?] trust their children to reappear in the classroom as normal, they are doing no more or worse than most employees and people in positions of authority in most walks of life: wanting to hear just the good news ; hoping for the best.

CARING FOR A DISABLED
OR NEEDY PARENT....7

Thousands of children are the full-time Carers for their parents; occasionally for their grandparents, as well or instead. They have to do this Caring because nobody else will. They have to Care out of love or pity, or loyalty or devotion....because nobody else will. Whenever Social Services or Barnardo's or National Children's Home hear that a Carer - insultingly called an Informal Carer - is to hand, they say "Thanks!" and set up a Young Carers' Group where once a month a child can regain bits of their lost, forfeited childhood. But that is mere tokenism.

There are times when parent and Social Services alike collude◇ in order to make tenable an untenable situation. In other words, society at large *needs* unpaid Carers for elderly or disabled citizens - and society is none too choosy about whether that child should be at school or not.

Schools *could* interrupt this cycle of exploitation - but they are often too kind, too tactful, too understanding, too admiring of a young pupil's sheer devotion to duty, to take any step that might part mother and daughter. They almost *expect* a schoolchild to be absent, or late, or too preoccupied Caring to do homework◇ as well.

CATCHING UP WITH SCHOOLWORK....6

Those people keenest on hounding truants, outlawing truants, punishing truants, are firm in their belief that nobody can ever Catch Up on missed Schoolwork - or, if they *can* Catch Up, they Catch Up at the expense of dedicated children who have never missed those lessons in the first place.

So, if the returning absentee, the returnee, is presented with too huge volume of Catch-Up, he or she might be deterred from ever returning◊, to the extent of truanting for longer. Or the truant might resign himself or herself to never Catching Up; to never understanding a routine or the additional classes laid on; thus needing to resume Truancy. On many occasions, the original Catch-Up has nothing to do with Truancy, just illness◊ or slow learning◊. But the result is the same : Truancy as a further escape◊ from Catch-Up.

CHILD SEXUAL EXPLOITATION [ORGANIZED SEXUAL ABUSE OF CHILDREN] [RINGS] 7

For years there has been a suspicion that out-of-control, off-the-radar-screen 14, 15, and 16-year old girls, in particular - usually girls - have fallen prey to Rings of (usually male) sexual predators. Some of these Rings have been sustained by the imagined or attributed lifestyle "choice"◇ of wonton and undervalued children who each welcomed the flattery, attention, cigarettes◇, drinks◇, and free taxi rides, given them by initially "kind" men. Rings have also flourished in several big cities because, with alleged or guilty assailants being ethnically of one background, the authorities - even Social Services - have been too terrified to intervene for fear◇ of being labelled◇ racist◇.

Even more sustenance for Rings of exploitative males, were it needed, has come from a widespread, and totally mistaken, assumption that the girls and boys drawn into their own rape, blackmail and demise are *consenting* ; that they are child prostitutes fully aware of the risks◇ they are taking. Another instance of :"blame the victim." Summon the Police back to base!

Almost by definition, victims or survivors of organized sexual abuse are truanting. They could not make their rendezvous without truanting. And their exploiters - exploiters often employed in the night-time economy - welcome *a daytime* stream of youngsters. Additionally, some children's homes, even some schools, have been less than conscientious retrieving girls they have already labelled◊ "complicit."

As far as numbers go, if the pool of survivors stands at 1400 in just one fairly small town, Rotherham - Sheffield, Derby, Rochdale, Oxford, literally, in hot pursuit - national numbers must stack up to a point beyond mere alarm. Representing a *catastrophic,* and irretrievable, closing down of childhood.

CHILD GUIDANCE CLINIC [S]....7

The Child Guidance Movement in England and Wales dates from just prior to World War One - and, predictably, it was an import from the USA. The notion behind Child Guidance was that certain children struggled both in the home and at school because they were "maladjusted" - or, not quite so pejoratively, "disadvantaged," "requiring support."

Naturally, Child Guidance would never have got off the ground without its accompanying proposition: "the dysfunctional household" freely supplying those "maladjusted" children to distraught schools. Advocates of Child Guidance properly see the Movement as excellent diversion from Adolescent Units, Pupil Referral Units◇ or the Youth Court◇ at later dates. Furthermore, keen advocates of Guidance say that many unhappy or underachieving children, also their worried parents, actually welcome the one-to-one attention they receive in Clinic.

Critics of the Child Guidance Movement object to the pathologizing of childhood, the medicalizing of child upbringing. Any miasma surrounding surviving Child Guidance Clinics extends to all Child Mental Health◊ interventions. Higher-end interventions include debriefing the post-suicide-attempt, application to Court for Parenting Orders◊ or Supervision Orders◊, A&E treatment for Deliberate Self-Harm◊, drug rehabilitation◊, and counselling◊ surrounding declared or undeclared sexual reorientation. And all high-end interventions suffer if that process merely throws together teenagers all with an identical problem ; or contrarily, throws together troubled teenagers each with a different problem. Is Truancy ever *not* a sign of "maladjustment"?

CHILDREN'S CENTRES....4

Where a teenager is admitted to Children's Centre or penal institution with education on the premises, it is reasonable to expect that Truancy would be impossible. How could a child go AWOL half way between one block of the campus and another? Of interest, "Care" staff and Education Centre teachers alike are rightly forbidden from forcing a child to attend education.

Alternatively, a Children's Centre might patronize usual or nearby schools for their residents - where, again, they are forbidden from forcing or enforcing attendance: another opportunity for Truancy on the part of a truant with too much on his or her mind. In any case, Young Offenders' Institutions have more complex problems and developments to address than missed education, consequential struggles reading and writing, hesitation speaking.

CHILDREN'S HEARING [S]....5

Round-the-table Panels run in Scotland, on non-adversarial lines, to deal with children going off the rails ; children perhaps in trouble with the Police; children sometimes beyond the control of a parent or guardian ; children truanting. Such Panels have been successful enough to need copying, replicating, in England & Wales.

CHILDREN'S REPORTER [S]....5

Reporters in Scotland are those officers responsible for collecting data, evidence, or perspectives, with eventual Children's Hearings in mind. Social Workers aided by *Guardians ad Litem* attempt to fulfil this work in England and Wales, but often with far less success.

CHOICE....8

The contradiction locked within the word Choice is that the journalists and politicians, and who trumpet its theoretical virtues most vociferously, welcome it least of all in practice. That is because Choice is profoundly threatening. The exercise of real Choice might upset many apple-carts and destroy many vested interests.

Choice matters in Truancy. And because Choice is sacred, it ill becomes anyone to castigate a student for exercising such important Choice / Lifestyle Choice, in respect of their education. In other words, every pupil has some Choice as to whether to stay or go ; whether to stay away initially, then go in later ; whether to go *reluctantly*, then leave at the first opportunity. And a big Choice, indeed a decisive Choice, is whether to feign illness in order to secure an extra day at home ; alternatively, whether to go into School despite genuine illness, so ignoring pain and discomfort.

Successive Governments, since the Forster Act of 1870, have sought to limit children's Choice as to the where, when, and if of their formal education. Choice has sometimes been too frightening an option to give somebody under the age of 14, 15, 16 or 18. Hence the laws that only gradually give young adults new leeway. Yet *Adult* Education, embraces, and thrives on, Choice.

CHOICE OF SCHOOL....7

Successive Governments have extended the sop of free Parental Choice◊ to include the right to state a preference for a particular Secondary School or Academy - even if it is of a different religious denomination, or outside what were once almost insurmountable "catchment areas." So now it is far from clear that Pupil X has come from School Y. Unsurprisingly, then, the enterprising truant can always claim to come from a different establishment, especially in Central London , or Birmingham, where campuses are relatively close together. And if a parent has opted - or been opted into - a faraway school, the disillusioned child might hate, even dread, the bus journey◊ there - and, once there, shed any residual commitment because none of his mates attend the same establishment.

CHRONIC FATIGUE SYNDROME....6

For those suffering it, Chronic Fatigue Syndrome / M.E./ Narcolepsy/ or the aftermath of glandular fever, it can be debilitating - to the extent of making classroom concentration impossible. All these drowsy, sleep-rich or sleep-deprived, low-energy medical conditions are difficult to diagnose. What underlying conflict, vitamin or iron deficiency, or thyroid disorder or idiopathy might have led to a previously healthy teenager shutting down or having to shut down. *Certain* it is that Chronic Fatigue must always be considered when Truancy or school avoidance is in the frame.

CITY TECHNOLOGY COLLEGES....4

Mrs. Thatcher's City Technology Colleges, facilitated by the Education Reform Act, 1988, were one of her ingenious ideas for increasing commitment to education on the part of disaffected, switched-off, pupils in Years 9, 10 & 11. Such Colleges were to be run more like F.E. than the Comp: with a curriculum◇ heavily weighed to vocational◇ subjects and interactive computer skills. CTC entrance at that time also brought kudos and some privilege. Doubtless the then Government saw great advantage freeing certain bodies from the shackles of local authority control. CTCs live on in Academies◇ and the expanding number of Free Schools.

CLASSROOM MISBEHAVIOUR
[CLASSROOM ANTICS]
[THE CLASSROOM JUNGLE]....8

Disturbance in the classroom is relevant to nearly all Truancy. Maybe the suspected truant has had a history of disrupting lessons: in which case, his teachers might be quite relieved at his absence. Or maybe the Truant was a ringleader, but has lost that status in a crackdown◇, so feels lost. Or, contrarily, the Truant is so disgusted at the bickering, shouting, petty-bullying◇, teacher-baiting, whatever, in class that (s)he decides (s)he has no wish to have further association with it. Or else simple boredom◇ might be the Truant's excuse.

Blame is very difficult to apportion where there is classroom breakdown - so the nearest or newest or biggest or blankest pupil tends to get picked out and sent into the corridor whilst possibly *worse behaved* children safely shelter behind that fellow's demise.

CLOSED CIRCUIT TELEVISION....8

The invention of CCTV has had numerous side-effects well outside school life. Where cameras operate at their maximum efficiency, they will pick up any truant or stowaway at the very moment (s)he attempts to skive off ◇ from a single lesson or a whole day. But the image has to be identifiable - not easy in the days of hoods and balaclavas - and there have to be staff enough to apprehend or arrest the would-be attendee/absentee in his/her tracks.

Then CCTV impacts upon the Truant at his/her *destination*. For instance, if a lad bunks off to a shopping mall, the mall's own camera might pick him out. And in the rarer instances a Truant commits a substantial crime◇ - or even a lesser crime, like urinating in a public place - CCTV may well reveal that misdemeanour first of all. Cameras tend to be more widespread - eg. on the top decks of corporation buses - than most punters, or pupils, imagine.

CLOTHING....7

Clothing matters to teenagers; in recent decades to 10-year olds too; far more recently, to "fashionable" 5-year olds as well. Clothing is gift-wrap to children : how they present to the world, and how they are presented by their parents / parent figures. Very subtly, Clothing is not the same as *fashion*. Popular, generic, chain-store Clothing draws on fashion - but is not considered quite fashionable enough by the purists.

Surely school uniform◇ kills off fashion - and the temptation to be fashionable. Not at all. School uniform can itself be tweaked and adapted to make it very different from what the head teacher thought it would look like!

Whether discussing leisure clothing, footwear, or "standard" school uniform, very many pupils feel excluded◇ from the world of fashion : but *included* in the world of the charity shop; *excluded* from happy Saturday mornings filling their wardrobes with exciting new garments. Moreover, the existing clothing of some potential truants is threadbare, torn, stained or worn out. That deficit deters many young people from even going out to hang about outside the local chippie. Being a teenager is highly competitive.

CO-EDUCATION....5

Co-Education's contribution to Truancy is possibly greater for the child who is transferred in from a single-sex establishment; and for the child who feels permanently uneasy in the company of the opposite sex. As with all aspects of sexism◇, so much depends on the gender◇ messages any pupil has already absorbed at home and from the cradle. Of interest, there is a greater correlation between Truancy rates and Boys' Schools than between Truancy and Girls' Schools, or Truancy and Mixed Schools.

COMPUTER GAMES....6

Computer Games are so accessible, so addictive, so exciting, so speedy: no "chalk-and-talk" lesson can possibly compete. Parents of gamers are often asked why they don't simply confiscate the console and block the software. But they are reluctant so to do: almost fearful that an angry◇ lad, bigger than they, might throw a wobbly.

The other aspect of Computer Games is that they are inherently violent. This violence either imitates the violence a teenager has already witnessed in real life; or acts as catharsis, so that the gamer does not feel tempted to go out and do likewise. The software definitely induces and persuades the participant to *keep playing,* to keep putting down the money : just one more zap. So the very "migraine" that allows the "authorized" day off school is aggravated by this quick-off-the-block virtual teacher.

COMPUTER GAMBLING....5

An adjunct of Computer Games is the potentially far more harmful Computer Gambling: gambling on and through and by means of the Internet. Either young adults do this on their own account, with money they have stolen or accumulated or gained by selling possessions; or their parents are so immersed in Gambling in their own twilight zones that there is not enough money left for food, clothing, bedding, heating, even less, for treats. Hence Gambling-diminished households and Gambling-loss, total loss, truants.

CONSUMERISM....8

Unforeseeably, more and more educationists are relaxing their views on Truancy : due to the tide of Consumerism. Consumerism dictates that consumer is king; that consumer should investigate 8 sites and choose a 9th ; investigate 3 energy companies and choose a 4th. ; have 6 motor insurers in 7 years ; and treat former state monopolies like the GPO and British Rail and BAA as ghosts from a one-size-fits-all past. Even clothes' shops are supposed to have 10 or 12 turnovers of stock a year in place of just four : Autumn, Winter, Spring and Summer.

In other words, if one can't obtain it on a price-comparison website at any time of day or night, it's not worth having. So it is that Truancy is the ultimate consumer choice: with a minority of customers - and the word "customer" is never random - deciding not to opt into *any of* the benefits offered ; voting No for all candidates listed.

COPY-CAT ABSENCES....6

As seen with Imitation◇, below, instances of Truancy: particularly those half-days away for snooker or televised golf or extended weekend - are likely to be copied. Indeed, one of the ways a teacher can detect Truancy, short of a flu' epidemic, is when 3 scholars are all absent in the same class, for the same double lesson(s).

CORPORAL PUNISHMENT....4

Although schools are rightly banned, nowadays, from using Corporal Punishment for Truancy - or as punishment for any other misdemeanour - this was not always the case. See Deterrence◇.

Unfortunately, Corporal Punishment is still alive and well in many *households*: especially where a family is less articulate, more conflict-centred◇, where money is short, and tempers explosive. Here there might be a policy of "hit now, think later." That should make Schools *extremely* cautious reporting Suspected Truancy to volatile parents. That liaison could, foreseeably, make a head Teacher complicit in a child's beating - even though he would normally disapprove of such a response. And it is puzzling why hurt children are so loyal to their parent-figures. How they hide their stripes, also their wounded pride◇Maybe some youngsters have never known anything else.

CONFRONTATION....9

Confrontation is an ugly and violet - certainly an unseemly - response to difference of opinion or outlook. In the home, Non-Confrontational strategies would almost always triumph over slammed doors, thrown china, shouting matches. Such strategies are wanted and not tried, not tried and found wanting.

Similarly at school, the less distraught and outright Confrontation the better. Why not ask the suspected truant to complete a traffic survey or clear bottles and cans from the school's playing field ? Or why not ask the school evader to talk to the rest of the class on the art of rod-fishing, the songs of Elton John, Spurs in the 60s ? De-escalation rarely fails . [see Amplification◇]

CONVICTION FOR ABSENTEEISM....9

Because Truancy is not itself a crime, any modern Conviction for poor school attendance tends to be directed at the parent or guardian, not the child himself/ herself. So it is that *the parent* who risks the greater fine or imprisonment◇ or disqualification. Even where a head teacher or school bobby◇ is on sure foundation, the Courts◇ might not merely rubber-stamp their proceedings. Quite possibly, most overburdened parents will be given some leeway or sympathy or second chance or revised target by Courts anxious to avoid a prison sentence. Even Care Proceedings - to the detriment of Social Workers, rarely at their instigation - might be preferred on the part of magistrates, by way of "diversion."

Nobody can ignore the fact that Court for Truancy erects a barrier to successful parenthood for parents and step-parents◊ and guardians who are already struggling in nearly every other department of their lives. Secretly, those bringing in prosecutions for Truancy might actually *regret* that decision, once an avenging agency's own failings are shown up in the cold light of day. Nevertheless, Convictions for Truancy in England and Wales rose an astonishing 75% by 2007, compared with proceedings initiated in the Year 2000. And the trend is still upwards.

CRIME [OFFENDING]....9

An outsider automatically concludes that truants must be Offending whilst they are Truanting - or at the very least, truants are they are more prone to Crime than their presentee◊ peers. But these assumptions deserve a thorough testing.

Anybody calling truants "Criminals" must first establish that Truancy is of itself a Crime and not a behaviour or a misbehaviour. Second, the smashed window lobby must explain away why some known offenders offend at night, when Schools are long closed. Third, they have to take into account school holidays◇ which provide Offending opportunities to everyone. Fourth, they must remember most offences take only a few minutes to commit. What are truants doing with the other six-and-a-half hours of their awayday? Fifth, if eternal vigilance is the deterrent◇ law-upholders think it is, surely there are far more detectives per truant out there, weekdays at 11am or 2-30pm., than on a bustling Saturday. Sixth, quite a lot of Crime is now done via the Internet, or from the back of a lorry, not essentially in school time. Seventh, there are waves of Crime *inside* schools : inside the very schools truants who have had their mobiles nicked are escaping from.

All these factors and features of Offending cast into doubt simple equations such as "truant up to no good," "rascal in the precinct," "lock your shed!" "thieves all!"

CRISIS....10

Truancy is not only Mini-Crisis in the midst of Crisis ; it also causes Mini-Crisis in the depleted classroom ; Mini-Crisis at Mum's workplace when news of the absence comes through ; Mini-Crisis at home that night, upon issue of a "grounding" order. In fact, Truancy is inseparable from Crisis. Yet, no reason to be downcast. To everybody's surprise, and no one's, Crisis in life is a mighty trigger for *change*; for change that would be absolutely impossible without a Crisis on the horizon. In other words, Crisis provides motivation and opportunity for persons and families unsure what to do next. On a much larger scale, some schools maybe need to close in order to be reborn a year or two later with new identity and rather more community support.

CYBER-BULLYING....9

Cyber-Bullying via Twitter, E-mail, Facebook, whatever, is not only quintessential to the unfair workings of social media and social networking ; it is also a *growing* phenomenon - and almost impossible to combat. Cyber-Bullying is, additionally, a behaviour impacting upon susceptible 8 to 18 year-olds to a far greater extent than any other age group. And it is those same top Juniors, early Seniors, Year 11 & 12 pupils and 6th. formers, who are most likely to access the social media several times every day ; also to self-harm◇.

For Cyber-Bullying to be effective, it has to be truly - and persistently - merciless ; preferably coming from

66

lots of directions ; nearly always anonymous; aimed at hurting at the victim/survivor's weakest point - weight, height, ginger hair, acne, B.O., too bright, too pretty, too clumsy in gym, beginning menstruation, whatever. The question then arises: "Why doesn't the truant/suspected truant simply put his or her device in the bin; not turn it on for a few days; not keep its battery alive?" Let it go! Ignore everything they're saying! It'll be someone else to-morrow! Sadly, all these sensible responses are impossible for most teenagers. Their i-phone is their means of self-validation : the object of their sharpest curiosity.

DE-BRIEFING THE TRUANT....10

The art of De-briefing the truant after an instance of Truancy is a vital skill. *How* it is done will determine whether Truancy will ever be repeated ; more fundamentally, whether student and parent can ever be left feeling good enough about themselves to ensure future good relations with the school / college where the absence took place, or rather didn't take place.

De-briefing must be *non-judgmental*. It must also be explanatory not incriminatory. Additionally, De-briefing must be relaxed, not hurried. To make matters more complicated, the teacher or school bobby◇ doing the De-briefing will have lost it if (s)he asks direct questions. Far better to open with : " Tell me a bit more about your day away...." than " *Where* have you been?" "What possessed you?" Any truant deserves not only the benefit of the doubt, but also a thorough and tactful exploration of those underlying troubles in his/her life: poverty◇, caring responsibility◇, anxiety◇, domestic violence◇, hunger◇, rejection◇.

DEPRESSION....8

Even where the concept of Depression is not brought into discussion around a child's Truancy, it ought to be. Better that Depression is a red-herring than that it is ruled out. Depression is such a big subject, deserving a book of its own, and it *does* impact directly on absence from school. Happily, most childhood and teenaged Depression is transient: here today, gone tomorrow; here in the tears, gone in the smile; here in the problem, gone in the solution.

Conversely, deep-seated or endogenous Depression is so serious that it now affects up to one-fifth of all teenagers, as opposed to one-fifteenth in less complicated, less contentious, times. Surely this must be a possible explanation, or at least a factor, when there has been school refusal or Attempted Truancy.

No way can the deeply depressed scholar get through a school week, school term, laboratory session or public examination whilst dragged down by demons. Nevertheless, thousands of depressed youngsters *do* survive against the odds ; do keep the show on the road; do reach uni ; do hold on to friends ; do disguise their depression, more or less successfully, behind loneliness◊, menstruation◊, insomnia◊, eczema, perfectionism, or bad temper, whatever gives cover.

DESCHOOLING SOCIETY....8

"De-schooling Society" was a bold book written by maverick polemicist Ivan Illich [1925-2002], published in 1971 to promote the disestablishment of education. Illich's central proposition was that learning works best when it is *requested*. Were teenagers, in particular, allowed to choose their own self-teaching programmes in their own time, accessing their own sources/ resources, they might learn more and learn it more quickly.

Without knowing they are doing it, truants *are* De-Schooling Society. They *are* exercising choice; at the same time learning in limbo; learning on the hoof. They have been given a menu where they have actually selected an alternative option to the recommended option; or walked out on the menu in its entirety.

Sadly, De-Schooling can never be rigorously tested - because it can't happen, won't happen, without brilliant Government Ministers thinking out of the box; without also, diligent researchers using a control group who have already been De-Schooled.

DETECTION....10

"Detection" is a strange word to use for Truancy, as Truancy is a phenomenon, not a crime. Yet even before the late 19th. Century, Detection had been crucial to the damnation of Truancy (the damnation of Truants too?). It is almost as if the Truant has to be stigmatized◊ as folk-devil◊; in order to hold him up as anti-hero.

Should attendees hear of the dreadful consequences of the act, they might not themselves be tempted to truant. Detection is always a multi-agency activity : Education Welfare Officer◊ working in harness with teacher in teacher's lunchtime, policeman◊ on patrol, car-park attendant, store manager, and foster-parent. And some captors of the wry are none too assiduous reading out a young person's rights; explaining that they are entitled to refuse a lift back to school; giving them time to organize a solicitor, where theft is alleged.

DETERRENCE....8

Any proscription, any condemnation, of Truancy or unauthorized absence has to have within it the power of Deterrence: setting an example to others. Therefore some publicity - whether in the national, local or regional press, on TV, in the League Table◇, or even on the School notice-board is invaluable to the law keepers. Up until the 1970s, alleged, discovered, outed or confessed truants were caned◇ : sometimes in front of the entire class or school. That too acted as Deterrent.

Modern fines◇ for non-agreed holidays◇; also Magistrates' Court fines◇ and prison sentences◇ - especially imprisonment - act as powerful Deterrence to wavering, anxious◇ or perplexed parents and pupils. Further than that, truancy patrols, and Police stop-and-search, are known Deterrents: either because of their visibility or where *possibility* verges on probability. Less obviously, an announcement in assembly that non-attendees might be barred from sport or field-trips◇ or the end-of-Year 11 prom, can deter occasional skivers◇. Or put all your suspects on litter-picking duty, second half of every lunch hour.

DETENTION....6

Detention impacts upon Truancy in two ways. Detaining a suspected truant in a supermarket, shopping mall, street, or trivial offender's house, is a highly risky business, one fraught with difficulty. Because Truancy isn't actually a crime in itself ; nor is Truancy an automatically unsafe destination or passing-through point. Better to release the able-bodied and street-wise teenager, pending the agreed inter-agency follow-up◇ to discovery.

In its other sense, Detention in a classroom for all of break, half of lunch, or an hour after-school, is a far more tightly defined constraint/punishment◇. School governors have to know what a school's policy on Classroom Detention is; and that it is to be fairly and rarely applied. On the other hand, a parent is not automatically entitled to advance warning of a Detention, nor has that guardian power to curtail/ or frustrate it. Even so, there is temptation for the recalcitrant to truant from Detention!'

DISORGANIZED   LIFESTYLE....8

Where a family is Disorganized : Disorganized in its getting up and off in the morning ; Disorganized with meals ; Disorganized in the laying on of help with younger siblings ; Disorganized due to alcohol◊ and drug◊ dependency ; Disorganized setting clocks, especially alarm clocks, Truancy may be the only and the inevitable consequence.

Very few children want to re-enter the classroom late: under the gaze of fellow-pupils who have arrived on time. And very few children can concentrate behind their desks when they are hungry◊, shabbily dressed◊, or weary after being up all night in a caring capacity◊ - or playing computer games◊.

This is where a School Counsellor◇, wise form tutor, conscientious Head of Year, or circumspect School Welfare Officer◇, might each usefully intervene: setting the actual or potential truant small, achievable and incremental goals. Perhaps start with a neighbour's knock-up call, then a simple breakfast, then a school bag / packed lunch got ready the night before. Or the charity *Homestart* could be brought in to befriend a lone parent◇. All this in the context of a multiply struggling family: struggling in every department; confronting every single outside agency - of which the school is but one - with a mixture of bafflement, incredulity, suspicion, or downright obstinacy.

Wondrous it is that so many disorganized children actually make it to their desks: in order to restore some order and sense to the physical and emotional upheaval they have just experienced, maybe experienced continually.

DOMESTIC VIOLENCE....10

Despite different campaigns, help-lines, mentors◇, panic buttons, posters, or exhibitions of "zero-tolerance," Domestic Violence happens, then grows, expands, diversifies, goes underground, ever disguising itself beneath bluster, congeniality and faux goodwill ; and perpetuates itself, free from impediment, free from reproach. Domestic Violence: mental, physical, sexual, monetary, however, never gives up, never owns up.

Therefore it is incumbent on every visitor to every well-functioning - or "dysfunctional"- home to ask the forbidden : " Is this a woman... ?" / "Is this is child..? too proud◇, too intimidated◇, too scared, too loyal, too browbeaten, too socially isolated◇, *too beaten up* to raise the alarm ? Many a truant is actually escaping◇ home more than (s)he is evading school. Many a truant is actually *staying at home* to protect his mother◇. Many a truant is afraid to go to school in case Mum will have flitted during the day◇. And many a truant has been up all night◇ witnessing the bust-up to end - *or, crucially, not end* - all bust-ups. And as if that were not enough, many a truant is hiding his or her *own* bruises, won during fruitless attempts to pull Dad off Mum.

DROP-OUTS   [DROPPING OUT] 8

Drop-out is a wonderful word picture because it instantly signifies exactly what is happening. If you do Drop Out, you are leaving the home or school or workplace or youth club you know and opting into a life and lifestyle choice far riskier, potentially far less friendly, with lower pocket money, and more fear◇ of the unknown.

Yet as long as there have been 14- to 18-year olds, sometimes children a lot younger than that, there have been drifters and Drop-Outs : NEETs,◇ sofa-hoppers, drug-runners◇, stowaways ; many young people with no label◇ round their necks - thrown out of wherever, lost, and seemingly going nowhere.

DRUGS   [DRUG TAKING]
[DRUG RUNNING]....7

Illicit Drugs - also the very harmful Drugs like Ecstasy: the so-called "legal highs" - wreak utter chaos and destruction; wrecking the lives of hundreds of thousands of previously healthy teenagers; in turn, overshadowing millions of families. At its simplest, a young Drug-dependent adult might be unable to attend school due to the need for continued snorting / injection/ stimulation / cold turkey ; or the need to acquire further Drugs ; or the need to come though a Drug-induced hangover.

More complex is the position of the young Drugs' handler / Runner. He - and it normally is a youthful male - needs to mix the Drugs he has just fetched and paid for ; diluting them by adding kaolin, paracetemol and flour ; then weighing them into polythene pouches ; in the same nocturnal session making the exactly correct bread-bag-with-peashooter equipment for inhalation.

This all takes time - school time? - effort, and strategies not to be found out; more to the point, not to be found *unable to pay* for the latest consignment. Seven hours behind a School desk might afford the risk of parental discovery of the scales, order-book and other paraphernalia. Additionally, the Runner himself might be needed on the site of *a different School,* for barter, preferential sales - and advice. All illicit or life-changing Drugs require a stream of new consumers....with money actually on them. So, short of Care Proceedings◇ or fines◇, what can be done?

Perhaps make the handling, possession and taking of most categories of Drug *legal*: whereupon the buzz, as well as the tight-rope, as well as *the reward* of illicit Drug-Taking disappears overnight. Meanwhile, *always* ask the unthinkable question: " Could this unhappy runaway◇ be caught up in the Drugs' culture?"

EASILY LED....7

There is not a parent or parent-figure in the land who does not say his/her child is "easily led" - at the same time having "fallen in with the wrong crowd." And these marvellous get-out-of-jail cards are almost always followed by the pleas : "Your Honour : I couldn't do anything with him!" " She never listens to me!"

Now there *might* conceivably be some spotless teenager, somewhere, who has merely followed the crowd as helpless tagger-on ; some young innocent suddenly pitched up against a hardened thug ; some hapless onlooker *forced* to join the fray ; some novice radicalized by a ranting imam ; some virgin totally unaware of her boyfriend's testosterone-fuelled promiscuity. There *might* well be, somewhere, a rookie glue-sniffer; or an untested, unworldly, party-goer offered her very first legal high; a youthful rambler suddenly finding a planted can of spray-paint in his rucksack...fledglings doomed to fall off the cliff.

However, even after being given the benefit of every doubt, there have to be circumstances where the excuse of having been "easily-led," within "the wrong crowd," lacks authenticity. Most teenagers are not neophytes. Placed under the most glaring spotlight, they are actually quite savvy: quite able to determine where to go and what to do, with whom, and for how long. In other words, they are both sentient and able to take responsibility. Fate is a terrible prospect - yet Fate relies on he or she who *tempts* Fate.

EATING   DISORDERS....7

There is a very high correlation between Truancy and suffering an Eating Disorder. Because their roots : low self-esteem◇, lack of nurture at home◇, lack of decent food   at   home◇,   poverty◇,   rejection◇, authoritarianism, whatever, are held in common.

There are three main Eating Disorders: Anorexia, Bulimia, and never actually consuming food or drink in the presence of another person.   And all three Disorders- especially Bulimia - are difficult to hide at School, even with the sandwich option, bought sandwich, packed sandwich: sandwiches frequently discarded in the Council's rubbish bin before school ever convenes for the day.

Thus EWOs◇ and teachers must be a little more *curious* in establishing the final link between Eating Disorders and absence from the classroom. The clues are there, especially clues in retrospect, looking backwards after crisis◇. But the possibility of the absolutely "impossible" - denial - needs bearing in mind and in everyone's observation and imagination.

ESCAPE....10

Without the need or the will to Escape, Truancy would be rare indeed: Escape from being grounded ; Escape from home pressures ; Escape from punishment◇ ; Escape from Youth Court◇ ; Escape from homework◇; escape from sports◇ ; Escape from bullying◇ ; Escape from plotting ; Escape from a particular teacher.

Escape works out fine for an hour or two, a day or two. Then Escape palls ; the very effort becomes a drag. Also the chance of discovery◇ greatly increases. Nobody can Escape everything for ever. The authorities are always more powerful than the individual. Inner demons persist. "Voices" keep up their torment. Tinitis goes unabated. Troublesome neighbours never get the ASBO◇ they've pined for; nor do they actually *order* that removal van. No Escape. Life affords few proper Escapes. So is Escaping worth the effort? Is Escaping the school, the school bobby◇ - everyone - worth the attempt ?

ESCORTED TO SCHOOL....8

The Escort to Primary School attracts little comment: whether she be mother, grandmother, childminder, neighbour, teaching auxiliary or taxi-driver. Only at *Secondary* School does the Escort become a consideration or a difficulty: because it is rather a rite of passage for a child over 11 to make his/her own way to class. Taxi-drivers will still be needed for children with a physical or learning disability◇. Otherwise, semi-independence is order of the day.

Laying the gauntlet down, some Magistrates' Courts◇ have insisted a parent actually *accompanies* an errant child to school, perhaps as condition in a Parenting Contract◇ or Parenting Order◇ as alternative to prosecution. *And children hate being shown up*. Social Workers are understandably reluctant to become that Escort, except for the newly-fostered child, on the grounds that *the child* himself/herself has got to assume responsibility for attendance sooner or later - so it might as well be sooner. Perhaps more useful than an Escort is the Meet-and-Greet teacher who puts a child who is floundering at his or her ease : especially the school-phobic◇ or the school-averse child who has been offered Monday/ Tuesday - Thursday / Friday education to overcome a disincentive, or impediment or chronic fatigue syndrome◇.

EVERYDAY SEXISM....9

"Everyday Sexism" is a fairly new term for the sex-filled, sex-fuelled, chat, the sexual denigration, the unwanted sexual attention, girls and young women, in particular - but also a few boys - experience each day of their lives, on occasions, a dozen times each day.

Girls are cruelly called "bitch," "cow," "slag," "slut" and "les," out of "fun": "Show us your tits!" "Two whoppers!" "Look at her bum!" And boys *do mean* their comments to be overheard - as do the builders on their scaffold and those commuters who ogle at the outdoor netball match. Up until far too lately, all these put-downs, wolf-whistles and slights have been accepted, tolerated, endured, as *inevitable.*

But these crushing and unwelcome interventions are no more decent, or bearable, than the Hen Party drawing up alongside a swarthy 16-year old boy crying out: "Bring out those goolies!" "Stiffen up!" "He's wanking: look at him!" In other words, Everyday Sexism is as punishing and as humiliating as Spasmodic Sexism◇ - sometimes more so - due to its grinding, unrelenting, frequency.

EXAMINATIONS / EXAMINATION RESULTS....8

Should a School enter a truant, or suspected truant, for Public Examinations ? After all, (s)he might not have learnt enough when (s)he was behind her desk to pass. And that could affect the League Tables. In reverse, a troubled child might be entered for GCSE but truant on the actual day. That surprise absence might be due to unpreparedness, menstruation◇, disorganization◇ - or fear of failure◇. Examination phobia is still a largely unexplored indisposition.

More commonly, children truant for *internal* Examinations and for mocks. Maybe, again, they fear◇ being exposed, being shown up, placed bottom of the class - or kept in a lecture theatre for the full two-and-a-half hours an Exam takes, with no toilet, no smoke◇.

Sometimes it is the Examination *year* that is the problem. In this instance, the rookie truant has successfully navigated the first three years of Secondary

School, only to be shipwrecked by the harsher requirements of passing Exams in Years 10 and 11.

EXCLUSION....10

There are two main categories of Exclusion from School: temporary and permanent. At half-a-million a year, Temporary Exclusions far exceed longer exiles. Temporary Exclusion is usually at a Head's discretion - sometimes after consultation with parents and the governors, sometimes not - following a relatively minor misdemeanour such as wearing the wrong uniform◇ - or the right uniform in the wrong way ; wearing too much make-up ; tattoos ; Mohican haircuts ; deliberate baldness ; fighting ; swearing at teachers ; throwing objects or furniture◇ ; refusing orders ; damaging textbooks ; carving desks, whatever.

The head teacher's hope is that the errant child will soon be brought back into the fold, duly chastened by 1, 3, 5 or 7 days at home; the hope (s)he might be doubly punished, or grounded, once at home. Every head assures his governors the shorter the Exclusion, the quicker the eventual re-integration◇; yet that re-integration might well depend on a letter of apology ; abject parental apologies on behalf of their child ; promises ; vows ; reparation ; face-to-face meetings with the offended child/teacher; or being placed on report◇.

However, Temporary Exclusions, like their permanent equivalents, fail through their concessionary provision of all those *extra* days at home : days off that *imitate* Truancy - in the process becoming a type of Authorized Truancy. For it is highly unlikely the excluded child will suddenly sit down to do 7 hours of Homework◇ ! Nor, necessarily, will excluded children work with their tutors and computers during every Permanent Exclusion. There is something very *isolating* about Exclusion. Some children - perhaps a majority - *hate* that isolation. Others embrace it as a route to freedom◇ from compulsion, graft, class work, homework◇, gym◇, the School commute◇, taunts◇, Tablet Withdrawal Syndrome....everything.

EXPULSION....8

Luckily, Expulsions from School are relatively rare: just under ten thousand every year, and not at all evenly spread across England. So the North-West of England, together with London, account for nearly one-third of the whole country's Expulsions. For Expulsion is a very harsh, heavy-end, remedy for gross misbehaviour. Those troubled teenagers - sometimes much younger than teenage - have pushed every boundary in order to be expelled : bashing a teacher ; bashing another pupil ; engaging in show-fighting ; drug-dealing◇ on School premises ; repeat refusal to follow teachers' instructions; bullying◇ ; sexual interference◇; rape ; an illicit love affair with a teacher ; insubordination to the head ; smashing School windows ; arson◇.

Where Expulsion relates to *Truancy*, it is again illogical: an imitation of Truancy, away from the classroom, left to one's own devices, free from all impositions or constraints: *authorized,* not illicit absence from the classroom. Also, Expulsion is very difficult to come back from. With no offers from a neighbouring academy◇ : total severance.

FACIAL INJURY [DISFIGUREMENT]....4

All young people are sensitive about how they look; and no part of the anatomy is quite so obvious, quite so influential, as the face. So if that face is slashed, burnt, disjointed, crooked, too unappealing to strangers - or left with a large port-red wine birthmark - the school child will really feel it ; and feel unloved, semi-permanently excluded from the peer group◇.

Furthermore, each child with an obviously different face will encounter bullying◇ and taunts and ribald "jokes" before (s)he even gets chance to come to terms with that Disfigurement. No wonder some school pupils affected, afflicted, flee from the classroom in tears. Yet those with distinguishable faces also make poor truants. They are simply too much in evidence: wherever they try to settle for peace and quiet.

[THE] FAILING SCHOOL....8

The concept - and reality - of a "Failing School" is completely alien to most teachers, educationalists and parents; also to most pupils. Yet "Failing Schools" were heavily promoted, and disparaged, by both OFSTED and the then Government from 1996 onwards. Which child would want it to be known their School was "Failing"? After all, school might be "awful" - but folk still come along for friendship, for gossip, for a welcome diversion from boredom◇, to feel part of their neighbourhoods ...but certainly not for "Failing." Doubts even exist about whether *individual* head teachers, teachers or pupils are *failures,* never mind their schools.

So-called underachieving schools "in special measures" are speedily propelled by league tables◇ and by disappointed Inspectors into a spiral of decline. First a good head teacher is sacked. Then other teachers resign or retire. Then lower examination results lead on to *even lower* examination results. No wonder some children truant on the assumption that : as their school is rubbish, they might as well rubbish *their own* hard-won achievements in the wash. Also it is widely accepted truancy has *its own* spiral of eighty-following-eight into the dell or along to the Rec.

FAILURE / FEAR OF FAILURE....7

All of our lives have been affected, also damaged, by Failure: Failure in examinations◇, job interviews, health, relationships, business, everyday tasks. And the Fear of Failure - as with all Fears - is almost as daunting as Failure itself. Fears crowd in more forcefully, rampantly, where unrest exists already.

In that context, truants and potential truants have, almost inevitably, experienced more than their fair share of Failure already: especially perceived Failure to attract their parents' or their step-parents' attention, approval and love. Also in the frame : Failure in sport, PE, and Failure to keep up with swiftly-moving computer games◇; Failure in the competitive sibling-group; Failure in any peer-group◇: gatherings where sporting prowess and sport-talk, sex and sex-talk preoccupy participants . Failure to love or to be loved.

Thus, a decision to stay out of the classroom - where everyone else has a smart-phone, their hands up, and their homework◇ done - acts as a useful firewall against further Failure. Where teachers and parents alike home in on a troubled teenager's *success*, whilst laying to one side any shortcomings - deficits which probably weren't very major in the first place - attendance at school could/should dramatically improve. Tellingly : success *does* build on success.

FALSE ACCUSATION [S]....6

Because many potential truants also have low self-esteem◇, a False Accusation - any False Accusation - whether levelled by teacher, head teacher, classmate, friend or father-figure, brings with it devastation. The subject of those strictures cannot bear the criticism, much less, the perceived injustice, that accompanies the False Accusation.

Then comes denial, rebuttal. And with any denial, denial has the effect of *reinforcing* the False Accusation being challenged : "He would say that, wouldn't he?" "Slippery fish!" "Lying bitch!" So it is that these False Accusations get legs and run amok. And, needless to say, social media, social networking, both get to work to magnify any initial Accusation, giving it an even more widespread currency. Amplification ◇in practice. Wicked gossip. Damnation of an already-depleted self.

FAMILY COURTS....7

When a Family Court is called upon to determine where a child should best live, with mother or father, aunt or uncle, grandparent or foster home, that Court must also consider school attendance. Nor should a hardworking, diligent, father or mother be disqualified from custody and access because a child truants from that address.

Although all Family Courts are *supposed* to listen to young people themselves and take their views into account, far too many Courts - meeting as they do under a cloak of total secrecy - tend to place more weight on the opinions of relevant grown-ups, visiting agencies, *guardians-ad-litem*, but not any children most affected.

And, very unfortunately, England and Wales do not yet enjoy the benefits of a single Family Court : *one* forum for adjudicating on child welfare issues, instead of a mishmash of alternative Courts and proceedings: Youth Court ◇, Magistrates' Court ◇, County Court, High Court, Court of Protection. Nor is there enough chance for young people to speak their own words in open Court. Solicitors are an important reinforcement of rights, but, crucially, their articulacy is second-hand.

FAMILY   HOLIDAYS....9

Family Holidays are now so inextricably linked to Truancy - counted down as "unauthorized absence from the classroom" - that it is difficult to examine them dispassionately. The case for the prosecution - literally- is that parents should endeavour to arrange all their Family Holidays to coincide with half-terms / Easter / or August, when schools would not be in session in any case. Further, it is alleged "irresponsible" parents take advantage of cheap deals, cheap flights, cheap accommodation: packages more readily purchased in, or for, term-time. And what of all that educational input a child will lose - forever ? - whilst sunning himself or herself on distant shores ?

Nobody can fully resolve this contentious issue because nobody can quantify 11 years' educational input, less so a lifetime's learning. And, arguably, Family Holidays are part of anybody's lifelong journey towards knowledge. Most foreign holidays have the capacity to teach language, dance, economics, transport, peaceful co-existence, migration, glaciation, the weather...so much.

Where parents *are* fined for their Family Holidays, they have to calculate: A) would their employer(s) authorize either paid or unpaid leave outside of term-time? B) would there be cover, or emergency cover, if a valued employee took a Holiday whilst School itself was on Holiday? C) is the fine imposed by a head teacher higher or lower than the discount offered by the travel agent / travel website? ; and D) will taking the Family Holiday - fine imposed or no fine - irreparably damage cooperation◇ and cordial relations, school with errant parent, stroppy parent with school, suntanned child with school, school with volunteer ? Surely: room here - or opportunity - for Alternative Dispute Resolution◇.

FAMILY INCOME....10

The importance of Family Income to the Truancy Debate cannot be underestimated or overestimated. Without an adequate income - and hundreds of thousands of families are *not* in receipt of a Living Wage - parent-figures are put in an impossible position: unable to afford the pens, books, sports' outfits, packed lunches, outings, whatever, that their children need to prosper at school, *and to feel included whilst at School.* Thus although an outsider might be puzzled that there is consternation about any child being without his / her own computer and smart-phone ; yet the child's pride rests on being able to keep up with the peer-group, and not looking down-at-heel. Until poverty-stricken families are able to claim all their rights, including money to feed and clothe school pupils, the truant or suspected truant will be heavily marginalized.

FATHERHOOD....5

Fatherhood may not be so obvious as Motherhood. Some young Fathers, indeed, do not know, or want to know, that they are Fathers. And recent changes to the school leaving age◊ makes it far more likely *Fathers* will be seated to learn basic maths and general studies. So why not harness all these young Fathers to teach their peers about ante-natal care, changing nappies, contraception? Where a Father *does* truant, he will probably given extra leeway.

FEAR OF DISCOVERY....9

One outcome no truant wants is Discovery. Discovery might mean not only a swift return to the classroom; but also the strong possibility of Head Teacher reprimand, later detention◊; worse, disgrace and punishment◊ at home. The truant who's good at Truancy does not get discovered - so street-cred also comes into play.

Discovery happens easiest in the pupil's own home/shed/attic, or behind the School's cycle shed. The forest is most difficult to sweep; the shopping mall also resistant to Discovery if you are truanting on a date near Easter or Half-Term.

Of course, if the truant is very unhappy in his or her own skin, very hungry◇, very wet - or very fearful of a rival gang◇ - Discovery will come as a blessing in disguise.

FEAR   OF   SPORT....6

Fear of Sport is a very real reason for Truancy. Maybe a fleeing pupil is not good at Sport ; maybe (s)he is afraid of being gawped at; maybe religious persuasion forbids Sport or the wearing of shorts ; maybe some rugby tackles , some football clashes in the past, have been brutal and intimidating ; maybe the runner is too plump or unfit to keep up with other runners ; or maybe Sport means surviving bitterly cold weather followed by a cold shower.

Whatever the Fear surrounding Sport, or not having the right dress or equipment for Sport, Truancy will soon follow - and for the *whole day* / half-day rather than just the Games lesson. And a parallel Fear is Fear of Sports' Talk : discussions antithetical to many outsiders◇.

FEEDBACK / POSITIVE FEEDBACK....7

When a pupil is given Positive Feedback: on a project well-done, 45 minutes in class spent obediently, homework brought in on time, bright appearance, charity fundraising, sporting prowess, whatever, there is terrific incentive for a child not to wander off. Presenteeism◊ overnight replaces absenteeism due to the process of self-validation◊ that Positive Feedback, even a smattering of critical Feedback, facilitates.

FINES....10

There are three types of Fine imposed for Truancy/ unauthorized absence. First, and most often in the news, is the £60 or £100 fine imposed by the school on each and every child for forbidden holiday◊, forbidden funeral◊, forbidden celebration. These fines, introduced by successive Education Secretaries, are extremely controversial; sometimes illogical; nearly always damaging to home-school relations◊. And not every school takes an identical line on authorization; nor are they equally welcoming an approach from an inarticulate, low-value, parent quite as much as entreaties from an articulate, *high-value*, parent.

The second type of Fine imposed on the "indolent," inadequate," "chaotic," or "colluding" parent is in the

Magistrates' Court◇ after local authority-initiated Truancy proceedings. Including costs, this penalty can mount up to several hundred pounds : behaviour often viewed more negatively because magistrates are either ex-teachers or very sympathetic to their local authority.

A third type of Fine is that imposed for Contempt of Court. Contempt might be the breaking of a promise to the Court to get a child into School, breach of Fines already imposed, or shouting out / otherwise disrupting the Court. Feelings run high; and nearly all Fines, of whatever type, hit families already in multiple difficulty rather than strong middle-class families.

FOLK HEROES....6

Were we to imagine what a typical truant looks like: bovver boots, a hood , a chain and a flick-knife would never be far away. Not a few conformist teenagers are intrigued by the Rebel◇, the hard-man, the one that got away (in this case, literally!). For the opposite of a useful role model◇ is the rebel without a cause, the cheeky outsider, the boy no well brought-up girl would ever fall for.

FORGIVENESS....7

In the sphere of back-street, even overt, money-lending, Forgiveness is an almost totally abandoned response. It is not in the heartless money-lender's or landlord's toolbox that he should ever simply Forgive, or absolve a debt which might leave self as provider short.. So it is with some families and schools: no Forgiveness. Revenge, or exacting due punishment◊ is taken as route superior to reconciliation, as if Truancy will spread like wildfire if not snuffed out.

FREEDOM
[FREEDOM OF THE GREAT OUTDOORS] 6

The quest for Freedom by all peoples at all times in history is heart-rending indeed. And from about the age of 3, children yearn for some a slice of that Freedom: Freedom to swop toys, Freedom to go upstairs, Freedom to zap TV channels, Freedom to play on the swings, Freedom to throw any food that is not appealing on the floor.

Unfortunately for them, nearly all children live in highly regulated households - or households where regulations appear fewer, but where those regulations that do matter are benignly enforced. In other words, there is no such thing as total Freedom for any child under 11 ; and where total Freedom appears to have been granted to *an older* child, that might be more through abandonment, carelessness, convenience, self-interest or default, than as part of a philosophical determination to promote Freedom in closely-monitored stages. No wonder even an occasional truant, or impromptu truant, yearns for a Freedom as tantalizing as it is distant. For it was *to be free* that God or the gods cut human beings adrift ; and took them off tramlines.

Truants especially yearn for Freedom from classroom constraints, Freedom from graft. And, unsurprisingly, that yearning translates into Freedom of the Great Outdoors. Just to be anywhere, everywhere: valley, mountain, beach, promenade, wood, lake, municipal park. Sadly, the *claustrophobic* atmosphere of school premises with their terrapins, their damaged Venetian blinds, their congested corridors and their suspended polystyrene ceilings, does not chime well with Freedom of any description: whether Freedom is *from* or *for*. And Freedom, like most ambitions, can be elusive. When the truant thinks he has found it, found Freedom, a mall manager, store detective, or school bobby ◇ takes up the chase. It is even possible for the Truant to get trebly rollicked: by Dad, the head and the copper.

FUNERALS....3

By definition, Funerals are final: a seeming inevitability, but *not* unavoidable. Despite their finality, and associated tragedy, not all Head teachers are sympathetic to Funerals. Some local authorities say children are too young to attend Funerals - so would benefit from attending school instead. Other Social Workers recognize the need for "closure" and for mourning, and therefore raise no objection to Funeral attendance.

Fines◇ for Funerals sound so insensitive as to be unbelievable, but fines *are* imposed on bereaved youngsters. There does not even appear to be mileage in *grading* Funerals in line with the importance of the dying/dead person : Dad above Step-dad, Granny over Auntie, Brother over Brother-in-Law. It all comes back to bonds of trust◇: trust easily destroyed amidst grief.

GANGS....6

Thankfully, Gangs, Gang mentality, and Gang revenge are not as common in most villages and market towns - most quiet suburbs - as in the inner-city, the ghetto, or the run-down, and de-industrialized, neighbourhood.

But where high-octane Gangs *do* operate, they are frightening; their methods and strategies brutal. Let nobody comfort themselves that Gangs are only made up solely of males, asylum-seekers, druggies◇, Yardies or Triads : proto-Mafiosi aged between 19 and 38. Gangs nowadays need to recruit much earlier: in the inner-cities, and need to home in on bored, disillusioned, 12 year-olds, girls not excepted, whose parent figures may neither know - nor care - about their teenagers' exact whereabouts. Tribal football fans are particularly useful adherents.

The Gang impacts on Truancy wherever it becomes the Gang norm not to attend school - or to attend school with the sole intention of causing mayhem, passing illicit substances and getting banned. Quite unconsciously, some schools *aid* the Gang mentality by both providing a distinctive uniform◇ and dividing themselves into Houses, sexes, denominations.

[THE] GIFTED CHILD....2

Certainly unlikely, but not impossible: the chance that a Gifted Child will truant. Gifted Children have very high IQs. Most very bright scholars *enjoy* normal lessons and find some fulfilment and reward therein. Just a few will be so bored that they stay away. Progressive Secondary Schools, of course, devise special programmes and tutelage for their outstanding pupils. That could involve giving the Gifted Child some teaching responsibility; also the sort of personal plan awarded dyslectic pupils.

GOING OFF SICK / ILLNESS....9

The relationship between illness - whether real or imagined - and Truancy is troubled indeed. Nobody really knows where one stops and the other begins. Illness would have to be verified by a GP were an employee off work for a week or more. Yet you can't really have infectious and under-the-weather children congregating in doctors' surgeries, cluttering them up.

Teachers must therefore take a certain amount of "Illness" as real, until proved otherwise. That need not prevent teachers charting "Illnesses" to see whether they happen more on Mondays or Fridays, more on examination days, less on P.E. days, whole weeks when strawberries need picking. Then how ill does a growing child have to be before that explanation is rejected in favour of recorded Truancy?

Another aspect of Illness is that its duration might make re-entry into the classroom daunting. Perhaps everybody's now on a different text or project or equation than before. Also, certain Illnesses like anorexia nervosa◇, bulimia, depression◇ and self-laceration◇ are not neutral. Fellow pupils are unlikely to appreciate the agony an acquaintance has suffered: agony that feeds into the temptation to truant.

GROUP - CALL....7

Group-Call has a lot in common with *Pubwatch*, Hooligan-Watch and Interpol. Here the idea is to draw every modern tracking device, every modern invention, every modern network together so that everybody knows what is worrying everyone else.

Group-Call will text a parent or guardian, or send an automatic e-mail, every time there is an unexpected or unauthorized absence from class. Even an un-swiped swipe-card◊ can trigger an alert. A variation on this theme is the landline call to the parent, where there have been previous concerns or Court proceedings◊ around Truancy.

Champions of Group-Call also extol its virtues tracing abducted children, lost children, and those who fall into a ditch or a well-shaft on their way to School. The onus is then on the parent to leave home or work and go in search of their missing child. Until they find her.

GUIDES FOR PARENTS....3

Some regional assemblies, and a majority of local authorities, produce helpful Guides for Parents on how they are expected to ensure, facilitate and promote their children's education; also what to do in the event of dispute or communications' breakdown. The current Scottish "Guide About School Attendance" is particularly clear, well-written, and available in Gaelic. The same is achieved with many a formal School Prospectus. Partnership is the essence: a popular word!

[THE] HELICOPTER PARENT....5

The Helicopter Parent is a fairly new arrival on the teenage scene. Here the notion is that a conscientious parent will so assiduously set her own GPS and her son's I-phone settings that immediately the boy is somewhere where he shouldn't be, the system will beep. Termination of lunchtime parties? Curtains too on excursions to see a new train passing through / a new store's opening ? The possibilities are, literally, endless for the Helicopter Parent who feels it is her responsibility to safeguard her offspring from *all* dangers, *all* potential downfalls: snares anywhere, everywhere. Including Truancy. Ensnared.

HOME EDUCATION
[EDUCATION OTHERWISE]....8

Home Education is a fascinating subject to examine : a beached relic of the 1944 Education Act which did *not* state that every parent or parental figure *had to* send their child(ren) to school : merely that they were obliged to put any child of school age *within reach of* a formal education. Thus a parent can still elect to stay at home and teach her offspring; or combine with the mothers next door and teach all their offspring together; or even educate a child in a caravan, on a boat ; educate that child in and from a specialist sports' coaching facility, dance school or theatre; or even send that child to the Library / computer laboratory daily. Nor does the Home-Educator have to be *a qualified teacher* herself.

Home Education is such a big movement / alternative lifestyle that there are all sorts of support-group, tutor-cooperatives, specialist web-sites, encyclopaediae - latterly all sorts of madrassas and Free Schools◊ too-devoted to its establishment, growth and prosperity.

So what of inspection? Obviously, the local authority retains the right to inspect Home Educators and their subjects. And, in reserve, an adult court◊ can be convened to try any parent using the right to Home Educate as a screen or foil not to educate a child or children at all. Or to abuse those infants in secret. Yet prosecutions - indeed inspections - are very rare. As with elderly persons' homes or health-and-safety, there might only be a one-in-two-hundred chance of being inspected, depending on where you live. For, by its very nature, Home Education is highly invisible.

Critics of Home Education are convinced home pupils miss out on so much : specialist scientists, artists, geographers, historians ; advanced interactive technology ; sex education◇ ; competitive sport◇ ; the best text books ; public examinations◇ ; most of all, social relationships; growing up within a peer group◇; happily uniformed; joyfully going out at 8am sharp 205 days a year; wearily, triumphantly, coming home on the bus◇, 3-30 pm. sharp, those same 205 days a year.

There is also the possibility that Home Education might become a sterile protest movement : protest against one school or one head teacher ; protest against the shortage of good, preferred, school places ; protest against being fined◇ for taking a holiday◇ ; protest against victimization or racial prejudice◇ ; protest against the school's dress-code◇ ; protest against RE or indoctrination ; protest against fixed-term exclusions◇ ; protest against past criticism of parents ; protest against Stranger-Danger videos ; protest against girls participating in sport or drama◇ ; whatever. Once Home Education springs solely from protest - however laudable and legitimate that protest - it sacrifices some of its validity, much of its potential for good.

HOME-SCHOOL RELATIONS....9

Whatever we call Home-School Relations : open days, target days, parent-governors, home-school liaison or Parent/Teacher Association, the way any school keeps itself informed about home, *and vice versa*, is vital to the understanding - *and reduction* - of Truancy. The aim is always for parents / step-parents to stop distrusting - or arguing with - school ; also to retain the engagement of semi-detached parents in the face of apathy, indifference or total switch-off.

Schools that are very good on Relations tend to let parent-figures know straightway if their child is away from the classroom◇; also gently to coax the self-nominated drop-out back. None of these Relations are helped by fines◇, by threatening letters, by unsolicited phone-calls to places of employment - nor by the sending of messages home with - or through - siblings.

HOMELESSNESS....7

Homelessness affects far more school-aged children than can ever be imagined. At any one time *50,000* lone parents or couples, *not child-free*, are thrown or propelled into Homelessness. By definition, that makes all their school-aged children homeless as well - taking no account whatsoever of their status as "children in need," also additional to a phalanx of single orphans aged 15, 16, 17; additional to single children in Care; additional to single dumped teenagers, NEETs◊: legitimately - or illegitimately - homeless in their own name, on their own account.

Homeless Bed & Breakfasts, homeless shelters, also inferior run-down tower blocks miles from anywhere, are *none of them* conducive springboards for formal education , for examination◊ entry - less so for returning to the school one attended before parental- or self-declared Homelessness. So it is that any Government *not* committed to automatically treating every homeless child as At Risk, should have that child's needs *independently* assessed, unhesitatingly given funds. Understandably, most Social Services' Departments are terrified of such an extended remit. Therefore the parents' predicament is visited on the child. The parent has eaten sour grapes. The children's teeth are set on edge. Worse, much of this "Homelessness," and very many repossessions, could be avoided by the simple device of turning unpaid or overdue mortgages into affordable rents.

HOMEWORK....8

Homework - particularly *too much* Homework - impacts upon Truancy in that the pupil expected to do that Homework might not feel up to it. (S)he might be tired◇, computer-less, or might live in cramped conditions (Caravan ? B&B ?) where Homework cannot be completed, nor handed in on time.

What better then than to skip the next day's lessons; hoping the teacher will have forgotten the issue of unfinished Homework issue by next week? Children without office-space or computers at home are always told they can go to the Library - but that might be situated some miles away from home, and be closed due to Government cutbacks. And Homework is a big imposition after a whole day of attending / commuting to school. Homework is often called the second shift.

HOME STUDY....7

Where teachers set work to be completed through school-originated, school-sponsored, Home Study, the assumption is that the pupil stuck at home will be skilled and self-disciplined enough to complete it ; thus enabling that young person to integrate better upon return◇ to the classroom. Official Home Study - as opposed to *homework* - is routinely set for ill students◇, those with severe impairment of their mobility, pregnant schoolgirls◇, children visiting the Antipodes, pupils suspended or expelled by their schools◇, and a tiny minority of pupils kept away because they have been denied a place in the School of their 1st., 2nd., or 3rd. choice. In addition, Romany children, also those whose strict religious adherence commands total allegiance to a mosque, a sect or a cult, qualify for Home Study - a regime even extended to children with tattoos, Mohican haircuts, or wearing strict religious dress not acceptable to the head teacher.

HOMOPHOBIA....7

Homophobia - which includes malign comments and retribution surrounding lesbians, bisexuals, and cross-dressers - is probably too vast a subject to be tackled in a Dictionary. Enough to say that several absentees from the classroom report that they have been called Gay, Les, Camp, Dyke and Kink " in jest." Better, then, a day in a garden shed, cave or friend's loft conversion than in the playground, having one's whole sexual orientation called into question.

HOSPITAL APPOINTMENTS / STAYS....3

Teachers are all too ready to approve Dental and Hospital Appointments where these have to take place in school hours. But if the appointment is for abortion, waterworks, or for repairs after deliberate self-harm◇, extra tact and sensitivity are required. No girl will want to go into detail about vaginal discomfort - nor will boys wish to discuss impaired urination.

Where Hospital overlaps with Truancy is loss of lessons, dereliction of the curriculum. It might sometimes be difficult for the absentee to catch up with the rest of the class. Occasionally a genuine truant insists (s)he has to go *with a parent or sibling* to A&E, chemotherapy, dialysis, whatever - where actual accompaniment of the other person is optional or avoidable. Again, a delicate area, considering the parent-figure's own pain, distress, and social isolation.

HUNGER....8

No student flourishes on an empty stomach. Yet the success (?) of food banks in the past decade - and their immense patronage - indicates how many children and young adults are turning up at School/work/youth club hungry. Ironically, *Kidscape* has found it is often the "ambassador" child who alerts the authorities that the *whole family* is operating on a bare larder.

Therefore every single truant or escapee asked to give an explanation for his absence should be asked also - asked explicitly - about Hunger. It requires our remembering: unasked children are *incredibly loyal* to their parents, and will not admit Hunger unless and until prompted so to do. Hunger is a stigma.

An ironic footnote to any Hunger debate is that one pupil in seven fully entitled to *a free* school-dinner does not take up the option. Such self-sacrifice appears nonsensical.... until the *pride* factor comes into play. There are still schools - especially in well-off districts - where the receipt of the requisite free token is very obvious, some of the questioning preceding token issue heard by listening ears. Even separate tables!

ILL SIBLINGS....7

When a Sibling is ill◇ - and where a parent-figure is occupied elsewhere, or is ill herself - it is up to the so-called truanting sibling to do whatever bedside duties he is called upon to do : emptying chamber pots, filling up the water glasses, turning over the sheets, lighting the fire, keeping the ill one company, whatever.

It would be callous and inhuman and reckless to leave an Ill Sibling to her own devices. Also dangerous. Where the young carer goes down on the register as "truant," he is fulfilling a vital role bothering enough that his brother or sister, stepbrother or half-sister, should get better. So why face sanctions? Many labelled◇ truants have enormous pride in their caring.

IMITATION....9

Imitation might be the best form of flattery - but Imitation is intensely disliked by teachers and commentators alike. All behaviours are imitative: but especially Truancy.

If a fellow-pupil or student sees that a truant has "got away with it" - maybe on a hot day, with world-class sport on the telly - the temptation◇ to imitate must be considerable: only reduced by the alternative scenario of being found out.

Some imitators actually accompany the alleged truant on his wanderings. Others employ the same strategies, and make the same "the dog at my homework" excuses, as their erring compatriots.

IN CARE....6

At any one time, there are 70,000 children "In Care" in the British Isles, scattered across 52,000 foster homes of uneven quality. Unsurprisingly, these children with so few anchors in their lives, so few reasons to rejoice, are over-represented in Truancy figures and most other negative indices such as imprisonment and self-harm◇. What an indictment on an *un*-caring society.

LABELLING....8

Labelling is a handy way of summing up the process whereby a teenager, or whoever, presents to the outside world as Goth, hoodlum, mod, rocker, dissident, young fogey, tearaway, tow-rag, big trouble, Jihadi, fan/fanatic, Borstal boy, whatever. The word-picture Labelling is taken straight from luggage-labelling or, more recently, from staff identity badges/ templates / lanyards. Also from World War II evacuations.

Sadly, some Labels facilitate stereotyping◇. Labels are also difficult to gain-say; to lose; to alter; to prove untrue; to find unrepresentative; or to offset against other descriptions concerning a truant/ young person's social and educational attributes.

LATE DEVELOPERS....7

Quite a number of suspected truants are also Late Developers. Perhaps they have never got off to a good start in kindergarten learning to read and write. Or a parent might have talked to self more than to pram. Or a child might have a low IQ, therefore need more one-to-one tuition than is possible in a class of 33.

The good news is that Late Developers *can* catch up, at least on essentials. There is a huge difference between "learning difficulty" and "difficulty learning" - so it's very important not to label◇ a hyperactive child as being "slow." Many very bright children - not a few on the autistic spectrum - cannot easily settle to deskbound learning - yet they are alert and knowledgeable on topics like supermarket bargains, fishing, the miners' strike, or Arsenal FC.

Where a Late Developer *does* truant, the age-old question comes into play: do spells of Truancy put the child *even further behind* with schoolwork: missed lesson content only fully recognized on his/her return◇ to class ? Some commentators concede Late Developers will remain late all through life despite any or every remedial intervention.

JILTED [CAST OFF] [DUMPED] 4

Most young adults accept that part of relationship-building, part of courting, is the risk of being stood up; the risk of arriving for a date and finding the other person missing.

However, there is an influential minority of young adults who are never reconciled to loss of a friend, being snubbed by a friend. That might be a prompt for injured pride◇, denial, jealousy◇, even lower self-esteem◇, anger◇, helplessness, hopelessness◇ or despair. Even then, for a few jilted teenagers, their response is brooding, driven, consumed by revenge. These are *controlling personalities*, so being dumped is a sign of loss of control. The cast-off teenager might only be able to wrest back some control by truanting from school, thereby, and incidentally, removing the chance of meeting the victorious ex, and sidestepping taunts from peers who'd always seen oneself as part of "an item." A separate, though relevant, concern surrounds young people dumped by re-aligned *parents*.

LEAGUE TABLES FOR TRUANCY....6

School League Tables have always been controversial: witness where schools for slow learners land up, predictably at the very bottom. And there is the big residual question of Value-Added. Value-Added rewards schools in deprived or struggling neighbourhoods which contribute to enormous improvements in skills and commitment to learning. Clever Schools can always massage attendance figures to make those missed marks appear "authorized."

When Truancy was first taken into account in the Tables, a Manchester School came bottom (top?) of the nation with 27% of pupils missing at least a fifth of all possible half-day sessions, the equivalent to 2 months of actual teaching and learning.

Once bruised and battered by a poor OFSTED inspection or a dismal League position, conscientious schools find it difficult to climb back up again. This in turn affects the quality of lessons - which feeds back into more Truancy. See Failing Schools.

LEARNING DIFFICULTIES....8

The subject of Learning Difficulty/ Difficulties is far too vast to cover adequately in a Dictionary. But Learning Difficulty can directly lead to Truancy. Anybody born "a bit slow," "a bit behind," "struggling to read and write," might be tempted, even prompted, to truant, if only on the simple ground of not making much progress when sitting there in Remedial English.

An important distinction needs maintaining between learning difficulty and difficulty learning. The two indispositions are definitely not identical. Very bright, lively, children might have difficulty learning once their minds are necessarily preoccupied somewhere else. And the process of learning requires a great measure of concentration: concentration being an absolute impossibility for those facing perpetual struggle retaining knowledge or instructions. If attendance improves, other literacy/numeracy deficits might still not improve. And a child needs a fair degree of attainment in order to begin truancy, avoid detection◊.

LONE PARENTHOOD....5

Being a single, or lone, or alone, parent is never plain sailing - though possibly a lot easier than living in a set-up where a dominant partner [usually male] takes more out of the household and its resources than is put back in. Lone Parenthood relates to Truancy in that a single parent-figure might be a lot more - or less - tolerant of a child's absences from school than would be the case if responsibility could be shared. And a less tactful Head of Year might *blame* the one-parent-doing-the-job-of-two for whatever problem arises in her offspring's progress. Worse from the point of view of addressing Truancy, the son or daughter not living with the absent parent - nor necessarily seeing him - might be tempted to stay off school a little more regularly in order to offer moral - and financial - support to the one parent surviving. On the other hand, family compositions are changing rapidly from past norms.

LONERS....8

Not every child is sociable. Not every child likes crowds. Not every child feels at ease in groups.

Education for most 5 to 16-year olds is delivered in batches of 29, 30 or 31. That can be quite intimidating for the Loner. So can having 5 boisterous siblings. So can the School Bus◇. By definition, Loners go it alone and maybe *enjoy* going it alone. And Truancy can be a very lonely pursuit.

LOST   CURRICULUM....9

No Curriculum is viable if there are not the students or subjects to take advantage of it. Sometimes Schools mean "Timetable" when they speak of Curriculum. More often, they become lyrical about the depth and breadth of knowledge their institutions are about to impart. Curricula are peculiar in that they always sound more impressive than they can possibly deliver. Just as no School would dream of saying it wants lower standards, fewer trophies, meaner challenges, unhappier children, so no School would dare say its Curriculum is not rounded: an ambitious mixture of Science, Crafts, Humanities, Inter-active Technology and Life-Skills. Nor can any School promise to include in its Curriculum *all* human knowledge.

In that light, the proven truant is bound to have missed out on part of a Curriculum - but which Curriculum? And how will that affect his/her adulthood and career? Ironically, most Secondary Schools compound the *incomplete* Curriculum by asking 14-year olds to choose 7 to 12 choice subjects for Years 10 and 11, necessarily excluding, straightway, all the rest!

LOWERING OF THE SCHOOL-LEAVING AGE....9

Lowering of the School-Leaving Age, LoSLA, is anathema to many parents, head teachers, and Government ministers. Would it be a reversal of all that has gone before? Would it be backsliding? Would it give the green light to all kinds of youthful misdemeanour? Maybe LoSLA would be an abandonment of high educational attainment? Moreover, could LoSLA place Britain out of step with other advanced or progressing (progressive?) nations.

Lowering the School Leaving Age is therefore a tantalizing improbability: never able to be tested as an experiment, because *never on offer*. We can only speculate that some truants, some school refusers, actually pre-empt any rethink by not turning up at school in any case. And the nearer one's age to the *official* Leaving Age; the fewer the public examinations◇ entered for ; the less Attendance Officers ◇ will vigorously pursue the *older* truant.

LOW SOCIAL STATUS....9

It would be wrong to typecast the truant as white / Afro-British working-class; but upper-class children truant, or think about Truancy, much less than lower-status children attending less highly-regarded Schools in poorer neighbourhoods. That is because more highly-privileged children have greater personal income, a better uniform◇, higher exam results◇, greater access to extra-curricular activities◇, more rewards for good behaviour and other benefits not shared by children and teenagers from challenging or underprivileged backgrounds.

Also middle- and upper-class parents are far more likely to pay for their children's education or to act as Helicopters◇: circling over their young ones, checking their offspring's movements, even their use of the internet - and certainly their school attendance. To exacerbate the difference, Mums with a patchwork quilt of underpaid jobs, other siblings to attend to, urgently, have less time to talk about school ups and downs; also about homework◇ and friendship patterns◇.

MARGINALIZATION....8

Nobody would drop out of School or out of a family or out of a community - or out of society - if they were not themselves Marginalized. The margins of any set-up are usually not very attractive: wastelands or no-man's lands, the true wilderness. So it behoves everyone *inside* the ropes to worry about fighters who have slipped out of the ring altogether beneath the ropes.

One remarkable feature of the margin is that it very rarely propels one of its new inhabitants back into the centre. Therefore the truant, for instance, once he has been confirmed by himself and his contemporaries as beyond the pale, stays beyond the pale. Whether dependent on bed◊ or alcohol◊ or tobacco◊ or drugs◊ or porn or earnings gleaned from the grey economy, the Marginalized, ostracized, young person often has neither the means nor the incentive to re-enter his school; no opportunity, less a desire, to even re-enter the (malfunctioning?) family - except to retrieve belongings.

MARRIAGE....3

With an effective school leaving age of 18, there will be far more married students in the classroom. Of course, not all married couples will be committed to lessons. More likely it is that boys and girls will *live together* before marriage : with the boy sent away, or at worst thrown out, from his home in order to live with his girlfriend's family - sometimes *vice versa*. Truancy might be a greater problem where this adoptive family lives some distance from base school.

MASTURBATION....5

A not insignificant proportion of boy truants, in particular, are such regulars at Masturbation that they find they cannot last a few hours, or minutes, without that comfort and resort. Maybe they have been overdosed on hard porn on their computers; maybe they have a natural - or unnatural - obsession with sexual fulfilment; maybe they need certain stimuli in order to reach orgasm; or maybe they worry they'll keep having stiffies in the classroom.

Absolutely certain is that overt Masturbation / flashing / cottaging is forbidden on School premises - whereas it is allowed, by default, in escapee settings. Perhaps an area very little researched: neglect intensified by the sheer (unconscious?) beauty of the teenage girls potentially sitting next to embarrassed - and day-dreaming - boys, 9 till 3.

MEDIATION....6

Mediation in Education hasn't been tried and found wanting; rather it's been wanted and not tried. Humble pie on both sides of a dispute is eaten in order for a mediator to be brought in: someone, perhaps the local vicar or RELATE volunteer or Neighbourhood Watch lookout trusted by both sides. Encouraging it is that alleged truants and their rather defensive parents / step-parents are all quite relieved to see a tricky bridge crossed. See Alternative Dispute Resolution.

MEET-AND-GREET....6

The person appointed for Meet-and-Greet does not have to be head teacher or Head of Year. That person might better be a *class* teacher or pupil mentor◇ or trusted friend. The idea of Meet-and-Greet is to celebrate actual arrival - celebrate in a low key, if necessary; and to reintroduce a pupil to lessons without fear.

MENSTURATION....7

When young women begin to mensturate - often at a far earlier age than in previous decades - not only do they undertake an important rite of passage ; they also begin a challenging and exciting journey that will not stop till their mid- or late-40s. All well and good when the girl mensturating comes from a wise and loving family. *However*, where that girl emerges from a culture or family that circumscribes women's sexuality ; which never mentions Mensturation ; where there is no spare household income for sanitary protection ; or where boys' "joking" about the onset or the time of month is grossly offensive, she will dread this aspect of puberty and be tempted◇ to truant on the relevant days.

MENTAL HEALTH
[CHILD PSYCHIATRY] 9

Mental Health is one of the largest and most important subjects to cover in a Dictionary. And because the Mental Health *of children* deserves an entire book - or library - of its own, all that is mentioned here is a summary of where it most impacts on Truancy.

Truants are not, of themselves, mentally ill. Truants might, in some respects, be more sane than their peers! Where there is a suspected truant with Mental Health difficulties, it is highly unlikely that child and his or her parents will be offered a specialist Child Psychiatry appointment for 12 or 18 months. Far too late; and an insult to the child, the parent, and GP alike. Mental Health is always the Cinderella when compared with, sometimes far more visible, *physical* health. An open question is whether time heals quicker than drug-therapy, quicker even than the talking-therapies. Amidst that debate, it is a truism that adolescents in general today are far, far, more likely to be officially "unhappy," "unsettled," and/ or "disturbed" than might have been the case in the 1970s or 80s when technological advance was comparatively primitive.

MENTAL TRUANCY....9

Mental truancy is an escape route essential to being alive. Practitioners of Mental Truancy learn how to sit in a business meeting, or on an organized coach-trip, or with their families in front of the TV, or at their homework◇ desks, with their minds somewhere completely different.

Despite the best efforts of adult trainers, adult educators, even *they* have never found a solution to Mental Truancy; so what hope is there for school teachers? Maybe ask the class whether they have fully understood everything up till now; but even that is not a guarantee. The hearts and the thought processes of certain children could well remain miles away. After all, there's a lot going on in the average pupil's life: playing sport, watching sport, romance, anxiety◇ concerning the future, hunger◇, whatever, to increase the chance of day-dream.

MENTORING....8

Wherever Mentoring has been tried: in Industry and Commerce as well as Schools, it has been fantastically successful. Children under stress might well trust a Mentor, perhaps a pupil slightly older than they, more than any teacher or parent.

That entails Mentors being properly trained; their having to complete role-play or practice sessions first; and their being able to offer *confidentiality* outside of disclosures of physical or sexual cruelty. Not only do pressurized pupils benefit from Mentoring. The Mentors also benefit. They are acquiring vital skills for the future - so their own self-esteem◇ rockets. In other words : Mentoring sensitively offered and provided, is a win-win.

MICKEY / TAKING THE MICKEY....6

For most people, even most *children*, Mickey-Taking is fun, part of growing up, part of siblinghood, part of romance, part of work-life too. And oh so harmless? Admittedly, some teasing must be taken for granted - but homophobic comments◇, racism◇, the use of words like "slut" and "slag," should be absolutely out-of-bounds; also teasing that has a nasty or sarcastic edge to it.

Not every young person is able to announce how Mickey-Taking has gone too far. It all depends on the level of self-esteem◇ a young person has built up already: a handy shield against anything the world might throw at her. That is why it is so gratifying to see teenagers taking selfies; using their mobile devices as mirrors! A *self-confident* teenager will not be caught off-guard as easily as the labelled◇ reject now bunking off School - if only to frustrate the bullies◇.

MISSED SCHOOL WORK
[MISSING SCHOOL WORK]....10

The question of Missed or Missing Schoolwork is vexed indeed. The prosecution always states that Truancy leads, inevitably, to lower educational attainment: on the grounds that absence makes the teacher fonder of *the Presentee*◇. After all, presentees present fewer problems with work-scheduling, if not with behaviour management, than absentees. Absentees require not only the effort of being chased-up; but also the effort of remedial or catch-up lessons, extra homework◇ set and marked...or the whole class slowed up when the teacher has to tell a recent absentee all that recent presentees already know.

In many senses, the labelled◇ truant misses a certain proportion of schoolwork and the set curriculum◇ *for ever*. In other words, the absentee for Italian reunification, for centigrade temperatures, for the history of Belgium, for crocheting, for egg custard, for pole-vaulting, for St. Peter, or for the writing of a cheque, will *never* re-capture the moment ; never know how Italy was formed, never know why Farenheit was inferior, never know about the German invasion of Belgium , never know how to crochet or how to make a custard tart, never understand the movement for pole-vaulting, never have an inkling that St. Peter denied knowing his Master, never be able to write a cheque the bank will accept.

The only trouble with this theory - at its most poignant when a spotty 14-year old renegade misses his lesson on the condom - is that nobody, not even the Prime Minister or the Pope, can know *everything*, or how everything works. Knowledge held on the Internet or cloud is bigger than any individual. The best any teacher might hope for is that *all* her classes, and all pupils within those classes, will be computer-savvy enough to be able to self-teach, self-learn, until their dying day. Which - while not making Truancy any less serious a subject for discussion - does place it in some sort of perspective. *Maybe the absentee is not ruined forever.* Maybe (s)he can be a success on the strength of the 88% of available education (s)he *did* receive, rather than that 12% deficit. After all, garlanded *presentees*◇ might themselves have been *mental truants*◇ for some of the lessons they were supposed to benefit from.

In addition, Missed / Missing Lessons also have the potential to detract from the planned schooling of ill children◇, pupils hospitalized or suffering from a disability◇, children on School outings◇, children not able to attend School because it is shut, or flooded, or frozen, pupils receiving an award at Buckingham Palace, pupils participating in coaching, counselled pupils, children made homeless or taken into Care◇ - or those entering industry or commerce prematurely. A true story is that a North of England lass was recently killed in a road crash the very week she was due to receive her 100% attendance certificate.

MISFITS [ODDBALLS] [OUTSIDERS] 9

To be a Misfit is to be placed in a cruel dilemma. One doesn't really feel acclimatized where one is; but if one *tries* to be accepted, one is still called a Misfit. And if one then requests a transfer, the new setting, or the new school, automatically knows one did not fit in whence one came.

The word Misfit is sometimes casually used, derived as it is from jigsaw puzzles ; at other times it comes across more stridently, when magistrates, legal counsel, social workers or the press seize upon it. So a *grown-up* Misfit can be anything from an eccentric to a convicted murderer, anything from a hobbyist to a loner◇.

The salient factor for truants is that they probably *never* fitted in at the School or the House or stream to which they were initially allocated. They may have had exaggerated difficulty with the transition from Primary to Secondary; or from Year 11 to F.E◇; or from London to the Industrial North ; or from comp to religious academy◇.   Or truants might judge themselves Misfits *wherever they land*, and in perpetuity. It is then the responsibility of parents and teachers alike to build up self-regard◇ ; moreover to capitalize on strengths ; to praise◇ the in-comer or out-goer ; to tweak the timetable◇ better to suit someone who finds arts easier than sciences, or *vice versa.*

One thing is certain: the alleged truant should never be *called* a Misfit. Instead, it should be pointed out that nobody, not even the late Princess Margaret or actor Kenneth Williams, goes through life fitting in with *everyone's* expectations. Everyone under-achieves, to some extent, and to some people's disappointment. Perhaps the saddest "Misfits" are *born* unwanted.

MISOGYNY....8

The pressure of Misogyny on young women, not least in puberty, is enough to drive any girl to Truancy. From birth, the girl subject, object, witness, or survivor lives in a climate of girls, sisters, mothers, being discriminated against, denigrated, subjected to violence◊, looked at in a lewd manner◊ and treated like dolls / sex dolls solely for men's and boys' gratification and self-pleasure.

Girls on school buses◊, girls doing sport, girls experimenting with self-presentation, overweight girls◊, the daughters of sex workers, black girls, girls in public houses, whatever, make up just a fraction of women on the *unfunny* end of Misogyny - and very little Misogyny is funny.

MISSING A SIBLING....5

Sometimes an absentee pupil has grown up surrounded and supported by Sibling or Sibling-Group. So that, when the moment comes, *absence* of a key Sibling or Sibling-figure begins a spiral of Truancy. Perhaps an older brother has gone off to University and can no longer look out for his brother or sister in the playground. Or maybe a cherished Sibling has been whisked away into Care, or into the absent parent's charge.   Quite often, the truanting child's brother or sister is ill◇ in bed, so needs some company and basic needs met.

MISSING A PARENT....8

Whenever a parent or parent-figure leaves home, even for a so-called amicable divorce, the chid(ren) left behind suffer loss and bewilderment.   Sometimes the child feels (s)he could have done more to protect Mum from Dad ; could have behaved better to keep parents together ; could have saved the partnership by never having been born ; could have said more about community unrest.

Loss might then be increased by a parent's hospitalization, cancer or death.   In such terrible circumstances, few children can make sense of what is happening to someone they love so much, someone who gave birth to them. So truants who Miss a Parent should be assisted with tact and sympathy instead of having the book thrown at them.

MIXED ABILITY CLASSES / STREAMING....5

The debate surrounding Mixed Ability Learning - as opposed to Setting or Streaming - will never be resolved. There are possibly as many arguments for as against. Where Mixed Ability impacts directly on Truancy is where the truant / suspected truant sees himself academically (socially too?) always behind and in arrears. He is never the one receiving his teachers' praise - because others got there first.   On the other hand, Streaming tells the brightest truant - and some truants *are* very bright and alert - that he is not felt good enough for promotion ; cruelly : he comes from a "Sink Estate" at home ; now a Tesco reject at school.

MOBILE   PHONES....7

In the early 1980s, Mobile Phones were the essential tool of Policeman, taxi-driver, drug-dealer, whizz-kid only.   It took some while for them to become inexpensive (?) enough for common usage : first for adults, then for 16-18-year olds; then for 14-15 year-olds ; then for 10-13 year olds ; finally for infants !
Mobile Phones assist Truancy in 4 ways: 1) they are far more attractive than school lessons! 2) their loss or theft sometimes needs Truancy for the retrieval; 3) they are vital for ringing school to give a convincing excuse for absence 4) they help individual truants and their genuinely ill◊ cousins to communicate with each other for rendezvous ; & 5) they facilitate crime: and disguise the crime that happens actually on the truant's watch, not infrequently, within the truant's *own home.*

MORAL PANIC....8

There is definitely Moral Panic surrounding truants and Truancy. Moral Panics actually precede the life and death of Christ! Ordinary lippy, boisterous, noisy, cussed, high-spirited teenagers are high on the roll-call of Roman Empire commentators orchestrating Moral Panic at the Forum! "Whatever will come of them - and us?" "Woe are we that the next generation is so unsuited to fill our boots;" "Who is there to follow in our noble footsteps....?" Truants are visible in their very invisibility. And where the Victorians boxed their ears and quite abhorrently thrashed them◊ back to class, our society dashes to court, so villainizing the escapee's parents and housing estates into the bargain.

MOTHERHOOD....6

There will always be school pupils who are mothers / or expectant mothers - but there might not always be young mothers in school itself! That is because some schools think Motherhood is catching, best addressed through private tutelage◊. Far better than parental leave that mothers *stay* in the classroom till about a week before the birth of their offspring; later also teaching their peers on all topics from antenatal care to labour pains, from the pill to midwifery, from sleepless nights to telling an overbearing, though fertile, boyfriend exactly where to go. There will actually be a greater number of *mothers* qualifying for extended education or training in the future: with the Government entreating absolutely everyone to get to work or to get back to work. "Hard-working families" all.

MOTIVE....8

The Motive to truant is everything and nothing. Society and parenthood alike can never accurately attribute Motive to any phenomenon. Nobody can know what is going on inside a teenager's head. So it is incumbent on everyone to wait and to wait patiently, to listen and to listen attentively, to watch and to watch observantly, till both Motive and motivation comes to the surface - as will assuredly happen when blame◊, and guilt◊, and embarrassment and despair◊ - also direct questioning - disappear into the wringer that gave rise to the very word-picture of hand-wringing.

NEETS
[NOT IN EDUCATION, EMPLOYMENT, OR TRAINING]....10

Very few neologisms or acronyms survive to become part of the English Language. But "NEETs" has stuck. In 5 simple letters, NEETs sums up a vast phenomenon:

as puzzling as it is intractable- impacting upon all Truants and *at least a million* young adults over the age of 16. That missing million : peaking in 2009 and 2012- but never seriously diminished before or since - represents such human wastage, unbelievable.

An extra dimension of the NEET is that, like non-conformism, non-fiction, the emphasis is in the word *not*. And that *not* is everso final, everso irretrievable.

Everybody expects some children, perhaps one in 100, to fall through society's safety-net of protection from physical harm, protection from sexual assault, immunization, health visitor visiting, nursery, whatever. Also, because *babies* are generally so cherished, so wanted, so much the centre of everyone's attention, it might be reasonable to expect them to be *equally* favoured 13, 14, 15 years later. Not so.

NEETs are inherently both completely anonymous and completely elusive; completely switched-off and completely unwanted: unwanted by almost everyone; despised and rejected◊. What led to this rejection of society, *society's rejection of them*? Drugs◊? Partying? An unsuitable, unstable, boyfriend / girlfriend? "The wrong crowd◊"? Bullying◊ in the classroom ? Bullying in the playground ? Bullying in apprenticeship? Inadequate parenting? Inadequate step-parenting? Parental homelessness◇? Personal homelessness? Simple sloth◇ ?

Whatever the cause or imagined cause, NEETs still slip away to sleep under railway bridges; to "sofa-hop" between friends; to live off their wits; to beg; to earn earnings through the so-called black economy ; to sell on whatever has fallen off the back of a lorry; in the extreme, to die in the path of railway engine or by jumping off a multi-story car park.

No Government is going to declare that it is giving up on NEETs - so mirroring those NEETs giving up on themselves, giving up on voting, signing on, registering with a GP or dentist, taking up their civil rights. So what is to be done about the NEETs and for the NEETs? Some Ministers talk of compulsion, definitely compulsory schooling till 18 or 19. Most Ministers speak the language of "toughening up" on youthful "benefits", withdrawing housing benefit for uner-25s, stoppin welfare payments and job-seekers' allowances that in any case have to be *applied for,* not granted as entitlement. Other Ministers simply wring their hands and comment more favourably upon those first-,second- or third-generation migrants only too willing to take up the opportunities NEETs appear to spurn.

NERVOUSNESS / NERVES / BREAKDOWN....8

It is by no means impossible for a teenager to suffer Nervous Collapse or a Nervous Breakdown, even before years of underpaid employment. Both crises should be taken with the utmost seriousness ; and certainly *not* dismissed as attention-seeking, or playing the sympathy-card.

Those who have experienced Nervous Collapse wouldn't wish it on anybody. All the nerves jangle, and clash in their interaction, and with each interaction between the nervous person and others. Peace and tranquillity seem so distant at those moments. Sometimes time out, or a wet flannel, or tears are correction enough. Instead, the misery, the jangling of nerves, the anomie, might last months, years. Any head teacher examining Truancy should also raise the spectre of Nerves and Nervous Collapse, as he would with one of his own staff colleagues.

NIGHT TERROR....4

Any school pupil affected by frightening dreams, hallucinations or Night Terrors will be unable to concentrate in the classroom the next day. Not a little of that Night Terror and consequent disturbed sleep◇ can be attributed to whatever past sexual molestation took place at night - or past abandonment, again overnight ; or bed-wetting, punished, bed-wetting unpunished ; or past domestic violence◇ so distressingly witnessed : much of it, again, after 10-30pm. Also poorer families are less likely to have enough divans - or enough dry bedding - to go round all the children. To add to insecurity at night, at least 50,000 entire families are put up in B&B, with up to 7 in a room or caravan.

Next day, school appears a bit of a distraction from survival - and not necessarily *a welcome* distraction. Many truants are really committed to making the whole indigenous family function, and function better. That tiding through, simply *getting through* to and beyond the penniless morn, has to take priority over formal lessons. Whole families find themselves sticking together through thick and thin, now committed to reverse sleeping patterns where night is for waking; 2pm onwards for missed sleep.

OPEN   PROCEEDINGS....4

Open Proceedings in all courts involving children / child care - provided there were certain safeguards - would be a really positive development. "Strangers" and press reporters alike are very *unlikely* to take advantage of Open Proceedings. We should all trust our courts far more if what they decided upon - to some extent, how they came to the conclusions they did - was all seen and put on the record. Ironically, most *parents* taken to court for their children's Truancy *are* tried in open Court. Openness is always less threatening in reality than on paper.

OPTIONAL   LESSONS....7

Making some or all classroom lessons Optional can actually reduce Truancy rates. Not much about education is Optional until the end of Year 9 - but then there are all sorts of exciting possibilities: drop German in favour of Geography, drop Music in favour of Advanced Maths. This sudden choice is available because no school can prepare all its students for every single GCSE offered by every single examination◇ board. Equally, no school can prepare all its teachers *to teach* every GCSE on offer.

So, while all schools begin to offer choice for ages 15 and 17, hardly any school lets its students opt out of *all* lessons - with the exception of all *religious education* lessons - and sit in the corridor or library until those lessons are over. Famously, A.S. Neill's *Summerhill* attempted blank choice: pioneering not often copied. Yet a realistic compromise would be some students setting their own programme for, mainly, computer-learning; or some students offering to teach their compatriots fishing, chess, snooker, model-flying. Gymslip mothers giving lessons on motherhood◇?

Two other versions of Optional Lessons have been tried: first, excusing troubled students from Wednesday education, allowing their survival through Monday/Tuesday, then Thursday/Friday. Secondly, a sizeable cohort of Years 10 and 11 in certain schools have are labelled "Vocational," deserving of "Vocational" lessons - and so are sent to Tech (F.E. College◇) one, two or three days every week: for hairdressing, plumbing or catering. The logic is that truants are far less likely to truant if they are treated like adults in an adult-learning environment. If they can see a tie between learning and earning. Over to Ivan Illich's vision of de-schooling◇ !

OVERLAYING IN BED....7

So disorganized are some teenagers' home lives, so many their harassed parents' preoccupations, that Overlaying is by no means unusual or unpredictable. Addiction to the Internet◇ / social media◇ /or the telly would *by itself* increase the chance of an unmonitored child Overlaying. And once the alarm-clock has, or has not, gone off, Truancy might be the only way somebody can deal with the prospect of yet another "L" in the herringbone register◇. It is never easy to enter a ready-formed, already engrossed, group if you're late. Even managers discover that truth at board meetings which have already started. Better sometimes to abandon take-off...with the additional benefit of an extra hour in bed, on top of the Overlay, to think through life's problems.

PARENTAL COLLUSION....8

To what extent Parents "Collude" with their children's Truancy is a contentious issue. Quite possibly, some Parents are ignorant of their children's whereabouts, therefore should not incur blame◇ merely for not being more inquisitive. Other parents definitely need their children around them, or accessible, to guard against violence◇ directed toward a mother-figure from a father figure ; to look after a younger or iller sibling◇; or to keep the family business◇ going.

And because parents are possibly the best judges of their children's emotional and physical health ; because it is parents who decide on the ultimate response to unhappiness at School : *withdrawal*◇ ; because parents themselves have needs, the charge of Collusion should be deferred - or, where proven, not acted upon till Parents have had a second chance. *Or even a third.*

PARENTAL MOBILITY....7

Modern parents are incredibly mobile: both between ready-made households and *within* the jobs market. Undoubtedly working away from home reduces any time left for surveillance, as does *ejection* from the main home. Sometimes one parent takes the child with him when he goes to work in a far flung place. Then that child will take time to settle - or to make new friendship groups. Or if Mum leaves home not to work elsewhere, but out of relationship difficulties, re-schooling younger members of the family might be tricky. A special branch of Truancy is that which is attempted between parent-swops, whilst adjusting to step-step-parenthood◇, heading somewhere not listed in the school register◇ yet to be updated.

PARENTAL UNEMPLOYMENT....7

One Government, perhaps unwisely, used "the closed curtain test" to drive a wedge between the "workers" and the "shirkers," the "strivers" and the "skivers." For reasons explained below, discussing Youth Unemployment, this was, and is, grossly unfair. Can a tree know the moment the axe will chop it in two ? Or can a coffin know the moment it will be lowered into the ocean? No more can the parents of truants know the coming of their dread redundancy notice.

And once a parent or step-parent◇ is without work, the *whole household* is impoverished, and to some extent stigmatized. That hardly gives the wavering child will or incentive to set the alarm for 7-55 the next morning for school. Shared hopelessness - shared helplessness - casts a darkening shadow over both the house and its former functioning: functioning that so depended upon income. Unemployment: worth always thinking about.

[THE] PARENTING ORDER....7

Where an English, or indeed a Scottish, court makes a Parenting Order, the authorities are saying the existing standard of Parenting offered a child is not good enough. So a faulty or defaulting Parent is expected to go to parenting classes and to avail herself of Social Work intervention until the point she is able to carry on good Parenting without the Order.

Parenting Orders are useful inasmuch as their very existence states the obvious: acknowledging as they do how every adult, however well-meaning, is not automatically a "good" parent : especially if she herself was parented inadequately. And many subjects of such

Orders raise their game significantly, and within months. That includes their enforcing a clampdown on a child's Truancy.

PARENTING   CLASSES....5

Parenting Classes make sense for a generation where birth parents and a whole army of step-parents◇ might not automatically know how to play with their children; with what foods to feed them ; when to insist on an early night ; when not to get angry and aggressive. Parenting Classes do embrace both *the origins* of Truancy and ingenious responses preventing its repetition. Currently, the Government and opposition parties all embrace Parenting Classes.

PASTORAL CARE / PASTORAL GUIDANCE....7

The Pastoral analogy: imagery taken from sheep cared for by their shepherd, is not only influential ; it is also extremely long-lived. Some schools have two parallel hierarchies: the academic and the Pastoral. The idea is that no child will learn efficiently while she is bogged down in personal angst◇, hugry◇, bullied◇, tormented, pregnant◇. Here the Pastoral Teacher or Head of Year steps in to help resolve issues - or at least some of the issues.

Good Pastoral Care in any school acts to reduce the instance of Truancy. Truancy, almost more prevalently: unhappy presenteeism◇, is nipped in the bud with a kind word of encouragement, some praise◇, some advice regarding difficult lessons, some offer of a pupil mentor◇, or, if that is the only way forward, every *Wednesday* away from the hustle and bustle of the classroom. Ideally, the Pastoral Teacher knows her parents almost as engagingly as she knows her students.

PEER-GROUP   PRESSURE....10

Teenage years are impossible to disentangle from Peer-Group Pressure. After the age of 11, *friends* begin to exert greater influence, and appear more engaging, than parents or relatives. Therefore, if a pupil's Peers are bunking off school, there might be the expectation a *non-escapee* ◇ in the friendship group might follow: so supplying companionship as well as cover. On the other hand, a whole Peer-Group Truanting on *one* set day is highly discoverable◇. Short of a mass epidemic of flu, the whole quartet/quintet will be in for the high-jump. Because of that inevitable detection◇, Peer-Group Pressure only tends to act as a *predisposition* to absenteeism; some acclamation once the deed is done.

PENALTY   NOTICES....9

Penalty Notices for Truancy / suspected Truancy are fairly new ; and amount to a fixed fine of £60 to £120 for each "proven" unauthorized absence. The idea was brought in from parking enforcement as a cheap and speedy disposal. Paying the Penalty is considered to be an admission of guilt: usually the parent's culpability as care-taker, not the child's culpability as escapee◊. There are also now controversial fixed penalties for shoplifting, even ABH.

Any parent taking her child on a term-time holiday◊- when that parent is not in one of the uniformed services- has to weigh up whether £60 is less than a holiday discount or recouped wages for unsocial days. And one entirely logical response to the Penalty Notice is withdrawing the child from class altogether◊.

PERSONALITY   CLASH....5

Nobody quite knows why Personalities Clash. Is it somebody's appearance or attitude? Is it concealed jealousy or unresolved rivalry? Is it lack of forgiveness◊ or lack of obedience? Maybe a Personality Clash arises, and is sustained by, memory of skirmishes past: almost as if each day is not a new day. Where labelled◊ truants fall out, or have fallen out, with certain teachers - indeed certain pupils - escape◇ might be their only choice.

PLANNED ABSENCES....6

Planned Absences are always easier to deal with than Absences which are unplanned. On the other hand, illness by definition is usually unplanned. Quite possibly, a child gets the date of her hospital admission date a week or month in advance. But that is the exception. Other Planned Absences are agreed holidays◇, agreed funerals◇, agreed family celebrations, agreed examination revision◇, agreed convalescence, scheduled Family Court◇ proceedings, scheduled Magistrates' Court◇ appearances, scheduled sports' coaching, scheduled theatrical performances, formal exclusions◇, formal expulsions◇

Head Teachers *like* Planned Absences because they are omitted from League Tables◇ ; also because they cause less friction between the School and the parent or parent-figure. Also the Head is given chance to advise on Homework or lesson catch-up.

POLICE EMBEDDED IN THE SCHOOL....6

In many cities and large towns, a Police Constable is attached to the local School - sometimes embedded within it, as if (s)he were a full member of staff. Where there is a spate of theft or rise in vandalism, that constable might decide to wear full uniform. On other occasions, plain clothing might produce better results : especially where pupils have suffered physical and sexual violence at the hands of another pupil. Embedded Police can never be a cure-all. It might take years and years to build up the trust of marginalized◇ or drug-dependent◇ or truanting pupils. The line must not be crossed, ever, however, that might indicate that the individual truant is an offender◇ simply on account of his or her Truancy.

POST-TRAUMATIC STRESS....4

Many children sexually assaulted by an adult or adolescent previously trusted as relation or friend ; many children sexually or physically assaulted by a stranger ; many children who have survived car crash, train crash, air crash ; many children suddenly bereaved of brother, sister, mother, father ; many children witnessing an horrific event: all suffer Post-Traumatic Stress.

So whenever a truant truants, parents and the authorities should ask first of all: "Could (s)he be suffering from Post-Traumatic Stress ?" And if the answer is Yes, no further action or retribution should be taken in response to that unauthorized absence. The only known "cures" for P.T.S are the elapse of time...and tender loving care. Mild sedatives *do* work initially - but are not an ideal solution. Bidding an adolescent to "snap out of it," or to "put it right behind you," or "to count your blessings," are all devastatingly inept. Even moderate P.T.S. takes between 6 months to two years to recover from, often longer: not too different from recovery after Chronic Fatigue Syndrome.

PRAISE....10

Truancy is so condemned by the Government that the actual person evading School is condemned as well, by definition: to add to all the condemnation he has already received for his clothes◊, his perceived laziness◊, his untidy bedroom, smoking◊, and the company he keeps◊

The opposite of condemnation, and the issuing of strictures, is Praise; and it has been proven how toddlers to teenagers, apprentices◊ to new squaddies, all *glow* when justifiably praised. That is the uplift they desperately needed. On the other hand, recent research shows how children are quite cute sussing out when praise is empty or over-the-top. Later, in industry and commerce, praised workers perform much better, and produce much more, than those perpetually subject to criticism. Praise is such a simple, reasonable, no-cost, and effective response that one is puzzled it has not been thought of before!

PREGNANCY....6

Gymslip Mums are cause for lively debate, anywhere, everywhere, perhaps through prurient fascination: "How stupid!" "How careless!" "She's made some tow-rag very happy!" "Got her Pill cycle wrong" "Should have gone for the morning-after..."etc.

And there *used to be* greater moral panic◇ surrounding Teenage Pregnancy. Mother-and-baby homes were opened; adoptions, some of them to Australia, were aggressively promoted; some local authorities even took away GI babies or all the offspring of 15-year olds. But that was before a raft of far younger Grannies offered to assist their daughters and grand-daughters with child-raising for the first 8 or 9 years.

Because society at large still fears the young Mum - and doubts her readiness for the task ahead - it insists that Pregnant pupils have lessons *at home*. Utter nonsense! It can be extremely fulfilling for the youngest young Mum to continue her education as normal ; at the same time telling her classmates - each holding the midwife's *virtual* baby - that " being caught" is not all it's cracked up to be.

PRESENTEES / PRESENTEEISM....7

If there are absentees from school, there must also be Presentees. Presentees are in one sense the fortunate ones : always there, even getting there an hour before the door opens. Presentees get certificates and trophies for their turning up through thick and thin. Presentees are also very easy *to overlook*. Nobody ever questions *their* commitment nor gives them the sort of one-to-one attention the miscreant / absentee attracts.   But Presenteeism by itself can be lid for a cauldron of *other* difficulties an escapee from home is facing. Mental Truancy, too, will still come in to play. At its gravest, the Presentee from age 5 to 16 might not have learnt enough from conformity for the challenges ahead.

PRISON [IMPRISONMENT]....8

Until the Year 2000, Imprisonment for Truancy was relatively rare: principally because Truancy itself is not a crime; also because Education Welfare◇ has usually preferred a softly-softly approach : gentle persuasion ; leaving the door open; rather than pressing "the nuclear button."   Additionally, the same local authority that puts a mother behind bars then has to provide all the mothering/ fostering itself !

And, as with fines◇, Imprisonment is intended as much as deterrent◇ as for punishment◇. The Government in the guise of the Department for Education now wants to send out a clear message to ALL ailing or uncooperative parents that Truancy will *not* be tolerated. Thus it is that scapegoated◇ parents, secure in their dungeon cells, imitate◇ their scapegoated children: the same pupils who were caught skiving.

PRIVATE   TUITION....4
Private Tuition - though relatively expensive - might be an option for the truant / absentee who has missed a great deal of schoolwork. This Tuition is sometimes money better spent when an external exam◇ is imminent. A useful alternative to coaching is provided when a teacher sets a special home-study◇ programme, one usually facilitated by Google and/or Wikipedia.

PROJECTS....4

Projects, at school, are assignments or dissertations researched, written and presented by pupils, with minimal reference back to the teachers / examiners who suggested them.

As it happens, Project-writing suits some pupils more than others. A lot depends on whether the young person has a computer and library at home. Yet for some disaffected or poorly achieving pupils, the Project is an enormous *obstacle* in the way of learning, an enormous threat on the horizon.

Therefore, many a young adult might skive◊ the classroom in order to skive the Project. Unsurprising that, when so many *university* students are also daunted in the face of their Projects. Answer : procrastination.

PUPIL REFERRAL UNITS....10

Pupil Referral Units are not always called that - but the meaning is the same : separate blocks, ideally built on spare school land, but more often a recycling of redundant school premises some distance away, where children truanting, excluded◊ or expelled◊ can come together, with expert guidance and one-to-one attention, to continue learning.

The P.R.U. model looks great on paper. However, in practice, four consequent barriers to effective education therein are insurmountable: 1) will the Truant actually *attend* P.R.U.? 2) has the P.R.U got access to all the maps, textbooks, computers, skills, sports grounds, studios that the local Comp provides? 3) do P.R.U. attendees so *relish* the prospect of one-to-one attention - where at real school it's 1:31 - that it makes reintegration *more* difficult, not less? and 4) does P.R.U. carry too much of the stigma of rugby's "sin-bin"?

Remember : many of those children misbehaving◊, truanting, or causing their own exclusion◊, yearn for attention at home, from the cradle onwards, upwards. Perhaps they have already had to compete with successive noisier, hungrier◊, angrier◊, iller◊, siblings and step-siblings - as well as coping with the witness and the repercussions of domestic violence,◊ and the aftermath of parental separation and divorce. So if P.R.U. is their *refuge*, P.R.U. cannot go on forever. Also, every P.R.U. still has to shed those nasty labels : "Sink," "Glasshouse," "Lock-up" "Loony bin."

RACISM....7

Insulting it is to those old or young, near or faraway, suffering Racism - or experienced Racism - to devote the subject only a few lines here. Suffice it to say, temporary and permanent exclusions◊ from School, referrals to child Mental Health◊ services, Youth Court appearances◊, YOI admissions◊, and Police stop-and-search are *all* heavily prejudicial to teenagers of different or mixed ethnicity, when compared with white working class. So it is certainly not a level playing field.

In reverse, Essex Boys, among young British males, are called "Chavs" or "Skinheads" or "Grebos" : so also becoming subject to Racism and racial violence. Just as white teenage *girls* can be hurt terribly, physically and sexually, following their being befriended by assailants of a different, perhaps Asian, racial background.

Racism directly impacts upon *Truancy* in that the already marginalized◊ child might feel that as (s)he is already on the very fringe of society, (s)he might as well miss school itself : where School has all the potential for ghettoization, the melting-pot for more overt Racism, - though most Schools are indeed pledged to combat that base expression of divisiveness in society. Are segregated Moslem or Jewish or Catholic schools really tenable ? - one wonders.

RAISING OF THE SCHOOL-LEAVING AGE....10

Ever since the Forster Act of 1870, RoSLA: Raising of the School-Leaving Age has been contentious. First of all, compulsory education was extended to age 13, then 14; then to 15 under Prime-Minister-to-be Harold

Wilson; later, in 1972, to *16*; then, guided by Tony Blair, to 18+: a measure that potentially puts married women and twice-over Dads back behind a classroom desk!

Raising a School-Leaving Age always impacts upon youth unemployment◊ - usually by reducing that figure by a million or so, overnight.   And always, it affects Truancy: when people who would have been *legitimately* away from the classroom in former years are suddenly expected to attend and to achieve.   That latter restriction is the more restrictive because RoSLA by definition happens to older pupils, those who have other earning and learning opportunities on their mind not catered for behind school gates.

RE-ENTRY / MANAGED RE-ENTRY....6

Teachers, parents and fellow-pupils alike have really only one chance to get Re-Entry of the alleged Truant to the form-room / classroom / laboratory right.   Better that no teacher, indeed no child, makes a flippant remark like: "Pleased to see you with us to-day!" "Stranger!" "To what do we owe the pleasure?"or "We always welcome our sheep back to the fold." Cruel.

Instead, the Re-Entrant should have a clear person or mentor◊ or place to go to at break or lunchtime, if the atmosphere or the pressure is too overwhelming. Then two-day schooling might be initially offered. This works on a Monday+Tuesday, Thursday+Friday basis, leaving Wednesdays free- so that the reluctant attender never has to face more than a couple of days behind his desk at a time. Better something than nothing. In other words, the Re-Entrant needs respect not pity. Neither censure. See Meet-and-Greet◇.

REGISTERS [REGISTRATION]....10

Although the old-fashioned herringbone Attendance Register is on its way out, in favour of swipe-cards◇, or automatic chip recognition, formal clocking-in or smart tallies, the *idea* of Registration is essential to the phenomenon of Truancy. Sometimes every single lesson attracts an Attendance Register - thus deterring spot or selective Truancy.

Some Registers are refined by having an "I" for Illness◇, an "H" for Holiday◇, an "SO" for School Outing◇, "E" for Exclusion◇ ; and , of course, "T" for real or suspected Truancy.

It is in no school's interests to have too many "T"s - as these appear on school League Tables◇, making some schools "Failing" or "Subject to special measures."

Even then, most schools still require a Register in some form or other, if only for fire drill. Registers are the foundation stones on which the whole edifice of compulsory education rests.

REJECTS [PARENTAL REJECTION] [SCHOOL REJECTION OF THE CHILD]....10

Very few people have difficulty understanding the concept of the Reject: the human "dross," the living flotsam and jetsam: beached when the tide has gone out. Nearly every "redundant" or "superfluous-to-Requirement" employee who has ever knocked on the door of a Labour Exchange has said: "I have been thrown on the scrapheap!" - and nearly every "jobseeker" firmly believes that to be the case, after bruising encounters with often heartless Job Centre advisers.

The Truant as Reject is even worse off, because (s)he hasn't even had the benefit of a few years of paid or voluntary employment. The Truant is Reject, and thus Rejected, rejected before reaching apprenticeship◊, never mind reaching adulthood, parenthood◊, home-ownership or financial independence from ageing parents. How society rejects the absentee from school can be seen in its reaction to trainers, hoods, mascara.

Meanwhile, in factory or supermarket, the individual *product* rejected is unceremoniously swept aside, then bundled into a trolley for disposal; in certain settings, shovelled up by the bucket of an excavator. Rejects do not have to be totally wrong; simply wrong enough to lose their appeal. So it is with marginalized◇ teenagers. They stop appealing to the parent-figures who cooed and chuckled over the cradle - only a dozen years earlier. Far too stroppy. And no novelty value.

RELIGIOUS PERSUASION....5

Religious Persuasion - inherent or inherited, understood or misunderstood - can weaken commitment to formal, compulsory, education. The obstacle might be one particular lesson on the timetable: sex education or girls playing sport. Or the obstacle could be a school's attitude to one contentious precept : segregation by gender◇, segregation by ability, segregation according to catchment◇, homosexual children◇, homosexual teachers, role play◇, Creationism, greens, whatever.

Religious or quasi-religious objections to the classroom are fiercest from some sects and cults: Scientology, Jehovah's Witness, Mormonism, Amish, Plymouth Brethren. - although there are many instances when schools go out of their way to accommodate fringe beliefs of every type, and to respect difference.

REPORT / BEING PUT ON REPORT....7

Most students get a school report once a term or once a year. But a few very special pupils are "Put on Report." That means they must hand in the head's Report Book at the start of every lesson or tutor-group session for that teacher's endorsement. When the head, in turn, thinks a corner has been turned, the Report Book is put away. Sometimes that same Report Book is useful for *single-lesson* Truancy.

REVERSE VIOLENCE : CHILD TO PARENT....6

There are strong indications the next big "taboo" to be brought into public discussion will be Reverse Violence. In Year 2014, 253 children under 17 were proceeded against for serious attacks on their parents by London police alone, compared with a figure of 207 just two years previous; and suspects were an astonishing *six times* that number.

Where an angry, bolshie, or disaffected teenager *does* turn on his or her parent, that parent's capacity to order their child(ren) round in the future, scoop them up and return them to school◇, is very much impaired. That specific manifestation of aggression - in common with the domestic violence◊ parent-to-parent, which a damaged child has probably witnessed along the way - is highly imitative◊ and repetitive.

REVISION BREAKS....6

So-called Revision Breaks for all Year 11 students from May 1st. onward, and for many Year 10 and 12 students *between* exams◊, are a persistent bone of contention. In Private Schools, paying parents despair of getting their money's worth. And in state schools, parents notice a gap between Revision *expected* and Revision for examination(s) achieved. Also and arguably, smart phones and tablets have made traditional Revision impossible, due to lapses in concentration.

Revision Breaks are best seen as a form of *authorized* Truancy. Such breaks free up hard-pressed teachers the better to catch up with the marking of younger pupils' work ; also for administration. Nobody really knows whether examinations are passed through genius, logic, method, memory, timing, luck - or by chance recall.

ROLE MODELS ABSENT....7

School children are not stupid. Their antennae are finely tuned to Role Models all around them. An important

Role Model is their first Primary School teacher - followed by first Form Tutor in Secondary School, their inspirational music teacher or head teacher, indeed.

More role models, so instrumental in limiting or eliminating Truancy, are parents / step parents◇ up bright and early, diligent, purposeful; youth club leaders; grown-ups living next door ; 5th and 6th. formers with brilliant exam results ; sportsmen and women ; or the classmate just awarded a hamburger voucher for 100% attendance.

The opposite of Role Model present is Role Model *absent*. Where a troubled child sees nobody, anywhere, setting a good example, there is no lead or leader to usefully follow - except into subterfuge; goods falling off the back of a lorry;   petty crime◇; internet gaming◇; staying in bed◇; getting teachers, school-bobbies◇, social workers, debt-collectors, whoever, off their backs.

RUNAWAYS....6

Whenever, wherever, there are Runaways: adult Runaways, child Runaways, offender Runaways, driver Runaways, there is alarm. Justifiably. Runaways are nearly always a risk, or at risk.

Truanting teenagers, by definition, are Runaways, or at least absentees. Maybe they are running away from cruelty in the home◇, unwelcome sexual advances in the home, from pregnancy◇, from gangland◇, from parental rejection◇, from child care responsibilities, from debts, from drug-dealers◇ from sibling animosity◇, or simply from a putrid atmosphere in the lounge, or in the school form-room. In such circumstances, everyone should hope and pray for teenager *safety* above all other, usually worse, outcomes. And *delayed* outcomes are rarely happy.

But the nearer the Runaway comes to his or her 15th. or 16th. Birthday, the less assiduously Police or parent-figures alike go looking for him or her. In that connexion, Police appear to have a *hierarchy* of disappearance: so that a "troublesome," "promiscuous," girl escaping her children's home may not be sought all that earnestly, nor the drug-running◇ black teenager based in Lambeth. On the other hand, the 13-year old child who has never packed her suitcase for exit before, never been subject of serious arguments and fall-outs, will prompt Police and search-party to go in pursuit.

SANCTIONS....9

The word Sanctions is distinctly unhelpful - as the same word denotes both allowance and forbidding!

The Sanctions - in the punishment◇ sense - for alleged Truancy are draconian indeed, not normally subject to appeal: fines◇, permanent exclusions◇, suspended or actual imprisonment◇.

That does not sound like giving permission! The trouble with any Sanctions, interpreted by successive Governments, is that they are black-and-white, allowing no finesse or mitigation. Whereas Truancy is far too complex a phenomenon for knee-jerk response.

SCAPEGOAT / SCAPEGOATING....7

The image of the Scapegoat is ancient and biblical. This is the ewe or the billy-goat led out into the wilderness to be sacrificed - in order that the wrath of God doesn't fall on any other creature. Thus, in the 1970s, sociologists included the re-born Scapegoat in academic parlance. For instance, Pakistanis in Northern mill-towns came to be Scapegoated by society due to a housing shortage they did not cause. Or football team managers have been Scapegoated for poor *squad* performance - even when the manager is not playing! Or company secretaries might be Scapegoated for a decline in profits much further down the production line. Or office juniors bear the blame for typing backlogs. Each *family* probably contains a Scapegoat.

Truants *do* actually make ideal Scapegoats. Because they are not *physically* in School, therefore invisible, Truants bear upon their shoulders the sins of anyone who is more visible: more misbehaving, less achieving, more thieving, less containable in the very classroom the Truant finds so oppressive.

SCHOOL BOBBIES....8

School Bobby is the old name for the Education Welfare Officer; and, like National Assistance, Supplementary Benefit and the School Board, the old name persists. Some parents are as adept and speedy diving behind the sofa *for the School Bobby* as for the foot-in-the-door moneylender or bailiff.

SCHOOL BUS....5

School Buses, well-managed, can be very joyful places: pleasant refuges during the intermediate minutes or hours separating home from school at both ends of the day.

Buses are where children practise their social relationships: observation, co-operation, sharing knowledge, learning about dress and make-up, sharing the social media, completing homework◇. Pupils commuting by foot or as participants in the dreaded "school run" almost *envy* those on the Bus - especially if there is the extra incentive of the opposite sex showing off - or a neighbouring School sharing the journey, arousing all that friendly banter and rivalry.

The *downside* of the School Bus, impacting on potential Truants in particular, is that not only does it have to be caught in the first place, and promptly ; it can also become a hotbed for nasty comments, swearing, mockery, violence◊, whatever. So it is that the sensitive or susceptible child feels bullied◊ and marginalized◊ before the day even begins. Then there is the dreaded trip back home - when bullies◊ have even more wind in their sails, enveloping darkness in their favour.

SCHOOL COUNSELLORS....6

Where they are appointed, embedded, or visiting, School Counsellors can be just the right point of call for each intending - or discovered◊ - truant. Named School Counsellors have an advantage over class teachers, step-parents◊, education welfare officers◊, and bussed- in Counsellors, in that they are mostly seen as *genuinely impartial* - also confidential : with the exception of having to pass on the disclosure of physical / sexual aggression. Counsellors can also seek a pupil's permission to approach parent / Head of Year.

SCHOOL HOLIDAYS
[HOLIDAYS ARRANGED BY SCHOOL] 7

What happens when the school itself organizes a Holiday of its own - or an extended, overnight school trip - *actually in term-time*? Because this *might* be the same School that fines◇ parents for doing exactly the same. All holidays are loaded with educational content, simply on account of all that travel, all those people encountered, all those places visited. Therefore it might be more logical to accept that parents, too, include some educational content: museums, shows, shops, sports, exposure to foreign languages in their extra-curricular holidays. That, in turn, is probably sufficient reason *not to* impose any fines on   holidaying parents and pupils.

Everybody remains duty-bound to congratulate teachers for their commitment and ingenuity laying on field trips, exchanges, ski-ing and archaeological digs. And in that vein, it is incumbent on society *not* to take away those School Holidays, despite health and safety considerations, but to authorize as well those overnight breaks laid on *by somebody else*.

SCHOOL PUNISHMENTS FOR TRUANCY....8

A raft of Punishments for Truancy are available to schools, completely separate from those Punishments available to parents and the courts.

Some Schools impose detention◇, with or without due notice. Sometimes, the erring child is asked to do extra homework◇. Many escapees are put on the litter-pick - or cleaning graffiti off desks. Hardly any single-lesson Truant evades being put on report◇. A final- and totally illogical - School Punishment for Truancy is exclusion◇. Exclusion gives the escapee far *more* free time at home: exactly why the truant truanted in the first place. It is all to do with the bond of trust / distrust the school is forging with home.

SCHOOL REFUSAL....10

The phenomenon of School Refusal sounds like Truancy - but on a far wider stage. The truth is that both states, although sharing some factors in common, have blossomed in different ways. The casual, or opportunist, truant - even the persistent truant - is making a conscious decision, then acting upon that decision; accepting education but not 100% attendance.

Whereas the so-called School-refuser (School-phobic being the more accurate term) finds it emotionally and psychologically *impossible* to enter School premises. Moreover, that Refusal might not be evidenced first in Primary School where, although a child misses Mum, (s)he yet might feel more accepted, more secure, than in the larger, more overwhelming, confines of the Comprehensive a couple of miles down the road.

School-refusers must never be harried or pressurized to return to the classroom - less must they be compulsorily escorted◇ there. The underlying amalgam of anxieties◇: anxieties not unfamiliar to agoraphobics, need addressing, and disentangling, first of all. Much later, there might be a staged re-entry◇ to school - even *a different* School - in the company of a mentor◇ : first, one day a week, then two. Patience must prevail here. On the other hand, the School-refuser / phobic must not be medicalized too early on. Room must be left for the proposition that Refusal is resting on (temporarily?) damaged self-image◇ - or hesitation to socialize, hesitation to answer in class, hesitation to do maths or science, rather than any deep-seated psychological indisposition. Labelling◇, as ever, remains significant.

SCHOOL   TRIPS....5

For most scholars, School Trips : to bird sanctuary, city farm, Roman fort, zoo or theatre, are very exciting. But for a few of their peers, School Trips are quite a problem. Have I the right boots? The right anorak? Have I money enough to give the teacher in order to go? Money to spend on the actual day ? Can I cope with getting up much earlier that day? No self-confidence◇? Hardly a wonder then that someone who can't afford the journey, and does not feel wanted, will truant on School Trip day in order to be less visible, preferring that course of action to sitting in the school corridor ; opting out, not to be a spoilsport, more out of sadness that no other department of life is going well.

SECURITY   FENCES....7

Far too little attention has been paid to Security Fences round   Schools.   These   enormously   expensive structures- running to half-a-million pounds per spread-out campus- are ostensibly to keep alleged paedophiles *out* rather than students *in*.   But they have had disastrous consequences on pupil morale.

The pupil experience is now that they are entering a guarded *prison* when they go to school. The only difference is that the Guard is a Teacher or dinner lady not a sentry / or armed soldier. Worse, the fences are ugly - and absolutely *not* fit-for-purpose because: A) the *worst* child abusers are usually relatives and friends known to families, not unknown men in plastic mackintoshes ; B) these Security fences have to be breached for public rights of way; C) staff have to park their cars and retrieve those vehicles at the end of the day D) many Comprehensives are *split-site* ; at best Lower School / Upper School a few hundred yards apart; E) Games' lessons; F) extra staff needed to do the opening and closing of security *gates*; G) drug-dealing◇ usually happening on nearby lanes and alleyways, not on school fields; and E) because unauthorized illnesses◇ are often a bigger problem for pupils *on the outside of* these lethal constructions than authorized exclusions◇.

Nevertheless, some teachers earnestly believe potential truants are kept *in* by Security Fences: as if a message is given to *all* truants by their erection. Even if that were the case, the Fences are unsightly and may benefit only the contractors that got the lucrative job of staking them out in the first place.

SCOTTISH LAW ON TRUANCY....4

In many respects Scots' Law is different from that applying to England and Wales. Northern Ireland's law is different again. In Scotland, the Children's Panel is very influential. It is that *non-adversarial* forum that will judge a truant and his/her parents first of all, in advance of harsher disposals available at a later stage.

The Scottish Parliament distributes a leaflet called : "A Guide for Parents about School Attendance" which starts with these words : "Attending and taking part in learning – wherever learning takes place – is fundamental to making sure that our young people become successful learners, confident individuals, effective contributors and responsible citizens. Scotland's children and young people need to be included, engaged and involved throughout their education. This booklet helps you, as parents and carers, understand how you can help to achieve this. The Scottish Government wants all children and young people to feel happy, safe and secure at school. We want to make sure children and young people receive day to day or additional support to attend school and engage in their learning. Parents and carers are by far the most important influence on children's lives and learning and it is parents and carers who are responsible for making sure their child is educated. "

Scottish Councils by no stretch of the imagination spurn prosecution◇, fines◇, even imprisonment◇ ; but Scotland does place more *collaborative* options in the way before the Children's Hearing which itself is less confrontational than an English court. As a footnote, it is possible to pick up a trifle frustration felt by some Scottish Councils with their law. For instance, Lanarkshire recently took 74 parents to Hearings for Truancy, only 3 of whom were convicted. One wonders how perceptions might differ as to who is aiding whom, and who is abetting. And what does the word "leniency" mean?

SEGREGATED SCHOOLING....5

It is hard to fathom the logic of total Segregation within Schooling in the early 21st. Century. Naturally, there will always be *partial* Segregation: depending on differing Churchmanship and artificial catchment areas. Total Segregation happens in Northern Ireland for Protestants and Catholics; in Oldham and other Northern townships for Moslems, Africans or Asians.

Where Segregation might cause, or advance, Truancy comes with the nervousness some children experience crossing frontiers. Such crossing is dangerous when dressed in distinct, tribal, school uniform◇; encroaching upon the patch of a rival gang◇ ; asserting white working class dominance when nearly every other pupil has distinct, alternative, ethnicity. The majority of Truants fail to subscribe to Segregation, rigid or otherwise - because they are already set apart.

SELF-ESTEEM....10

Self-Esteem is so fundamental to all afflictions of childhood; and those who study the behaviour of children and teenagers know that its wide reach can neither be underestimated or overestimated.

Low Self-Esteem leads Truants not to value themselves enough to see that teachers and other pupils - also their own families - *like* them, and are rooting for them. Build up that Self-Image - boost it in every way possible through art, drama, outdoor pursuits, whatever- and unauthorized absences from school might be fewer.

SELF-HARM
[DELIBERATE SELF-HARM] 9

The link between Truancy and Self-Harm is both acknowledged and cause for bafflement and horror. Because *all* Self-Harm is horrifying : self-flagellation, head-banging, self-laceration, disembowelling, piercing, pulling one's hair out, scabbing. Do young people accused of truanting Self-Harm *before* bunking off School, or *during* their unscheduled absences? And why do some Self-Harmers - maybe the majority - *continue* regular attendance ? Perhaps it's all to do with *concealment*. A Truant has in a way busted his flush. Nonetheless, if you're not at School, your cuts will not be seen by anybody; your tears of agony not heard by anybody. And it is the same cluster of distresses that lead to Self-Harm that carry forward to much Truancy.

The jury is still out as to whether Deliberate Self-Harm is escape◇, escapism, or the opposite: facing *reality*.

SELF-EDUCATION PROGRAMMES....5

Examination◇ revision is nothing if it is not a Self-Education Programme. Much Googling on the computer; much consumption of You Tube and Wikipedia ; indeed, much set Homework◇; much reading of library-books for pleasure : all these, too, count as Self-Education. Logically, it is also possible that Truancy is gateway to Self-Education. Many long-term patients on the Children's Ward of the local Infirmary; many young people excluded◇ or expelled◇ from school ; many gifted children◇ ; also many budding linguists and musicians, are set specific Self-Education tapes, books and multiple-choice questionnaires. Self-Education might even be a condition of examination◇ re-entry, certainly for going up a Maths' division.

SELF-VALIDATION....10

Nobody is anybody without Self-Validation. In turn, that Validation has to be mirrored and reflected back through parents, teachers or friends - if only because it is *highly unlikely* a child or teenager will wake up one morning and exclaim: "I am Valid!" Most young adults, thankfully, *are* Validated. Society, along with its schools - would be infinitely poorer were teenagers not both Validated *and* praised◇. Ideally, birth alone should be some Validation. But in *dysfunctional* families◇, that very birth might be counted as imposition, or negation. No self-respecting person should have *to apologize* for having been born (nor sacrifice their Child Benefit for being a fourth birth!). Intending truants are ambassadors of a type, searching for Validation *outside* school, possibly with older peer-groups◇.

SETTING AN EXAMPLE
[MAKING AN EXAMPLE]....6

When the Truant of 1965 was caned in front of the whole class / whole school, an example was certainly set for others. Nowadays, exclusions◇, expulsions◇ and, especially, high parental fines◇, long prison sentences◇, are all meant to distract or restrain - or to warn - others: other children about to absent themselves, other parents about to aid and abet their children's unauthorized absences.

SEX EDUCATION....5

Often pointed out to parents and Truants is that they have missed their Sex Education lesson. That is to assume that they never had such a lesson by chance, from their peer-group◇, via mobile phone◇ or pornography, worse : in the process of being groomed and sexually molested by friends, relatives or people in positions of responsibility whom they had trusted or been encouraged to place their faith in.

The best Sex Education is very daring: using real life models, actual film, bold question-and-answer sessions, experiential role-play◇. Therefore most Schools still fight shy of the best they could have provided, imagining they on thin ice with parents or the - conservative - local authority. Why not rely on some of the best Sex Education, offered by heavily pregnant or newly delivered 14-, 15-, or 16-year old School friends?

How illogical then that pregnant◇ girls are traditionally *excluded from*◇ the classroom, and home-educated◇. Better that everybody shares the experience of being prematurely tied down, burdened, exercised, exhilarated, validated, with each gymslip Mum, with each proud boyfriend / itinerant father◇.

SEXISM / GENDER DISCRIMINATION....8

Sexism is endemic in education, despite some Governors', politicians,' and selectors' best endeavours:

perhaps made worse by the existence of single-sex Schools◊. There is nothing wrong with co-education◊; indeed Girls' Schools have given a huge lift to girl achievers, girl scientists, girl examinees in particular; but singularity only puts off the day girls have to encounter boys in young adulthood; and boys sometimes prosper when they encounter "swotting" girls. And nobody should forger that male pupils, also, experience Sexism. For instance, boys are not naturally directed towards netball, domestic science, teen-mags and the pre-natal clinic.

As a society we rarely ask girls whether they are truanting - or fearing School - *because of their womanhood*. Schoolgirls are probably called "sluts" or "slags," leses" or "tarts" dozens of times a week - and marginalized◊ in the playground. Co-education simply provides a different theatre for this gross behaviour, these dreadful insults.

SHELTERING THE TRUANT....9

Of necessity, every truant or suspected truant needs a shelter: for 7 hours on any one day, many days in succession. One does not have to be a brilliant detective to know that Shelter is more likely in a child's own home or in the home of a close friend: perhaps the refuge for a friend bunking off in concert. Homes might well be safer than streets, forests or deserted warehouses.

The enterprising truant uses a loft or an out-house - or else hides under the bed when the School Bobby◇ calls. Alternative shelters for the truant are shopping mall, allotment shed, closed factory, or Church left unattended for private worship! Shelter-keepers may provide - or deny - an alibi; coerce the truant back to school, or let him go.

SHIELDING....8

It is hard on a busy, or oppressed, or multiply-disabled, or health-obsessed parent figure to be accused of Shielding her truanting child, or Shielding a son's best friend also suspected of truanting.

Society expects the shield. That is what every film about every criminal, every runaway◇, offers a front-man or look-out, someone engaged to mislead the authorities, or to protest "innocence" as accomplice. Ironically, shielders of escapees◇ are often convinced they are helping a child wilting under pressure. After all, only a parent-figure has access to everything that's influenced a child's upbringing, up until 24 hours ago.

SIBLING   ENVY....6

Not a few Schools risk alienating Siblings / Step-Siblings by saying: " You must be Angela's brother ! Now Angela was our star pupil !" "Your Silvester's going to be a hard act to follow!" - for thereby they are unconsciously laying down the foundation for the other Sibling(s) to feel hopelessly inadequate.

Teenage boys, in any case, tend to lag behind extremely bright girls of the same age. So not a few children experiencing Sibling-Envy bunk off from the very school where they might perceive themselves as failures◊, or not quite good enough.

[THE]   SKILLS'   SHORTAGE....7

All industry, most commerce, and many Government ministers, complain about a national / regional/ scientific Skills' Shortage.   These are people who tolerate - indeed, almost welcome - some youth unemployment◊, yet pine for a set of school-leavers, graduates and job candidates with *skills* : ICT, engineering, physics, numeracy, experiment, analysis, construction, mechanics, micro-biology, whatever.

Now that *should* provide the push, the impetus, for marrying truants and Neets◇ with a Skills' Shortage which has, hitherto, been most associated with the migrants from other countries who come and fill it. Were disillusioned, switched-off, yet able, potential truants packed off at the age of 11 or 12 to acquire all the skills the nation *thought* it was short of: first, those alienated◇ young people would feel valued ; second, they'd see a link between learning and earning ; third, they'd have the security of a future income; fourth, and crucially, they'd have less motive to beat the system that, before any debate

.

SINGLING   OUT....7

Being Singled Out is a fascinating, though sometimes upsetting, process. Some people *love* being Singled Out: the top athlete, the class swot, the budding pianist, the champion rower. Without their being Singled Out, such high-achievers might descend into obscurity. Yet other grown-ups, other children, do *not* want to be Singled Out, because such selectivity is threatening. Better to be one of the crowd, one of the rabble: suitably anonymous, disguised, overlooked. And to make matters more complicated - were that possible - not a few children or employees *wish to be* Singled Out some days, then hidden on other days ; in bog-standard jeans one day, dressed to the nines a week later; on the terraces one Saturday, team mascot the following Saturday.

The truant's experience of being Single Out is an equally complex mix. He may well truant because he was once (unnervingly?) Singled Out by his class teacher or his head teacher when he still felt some attachment to the classroom. Then, once on the run, the last thing the truant wanted was Singling Out! In order to sustain his new lifestyle, many a truant needs not to be on a store detective or security officer's radar; and certainly not the only hitchhiker on the roadside; nor the only wanderer in a deserted public park; the only skateboarder on the piazza.

SKIPPING....by definition
see Bunking Off

SKIVING....by defintion.   See Bunking Off.

SMOKING....7

Teenagers, sometimes much younger children, are five times more likely to take up Smoking if they see their parent / parent-figure Smoking than if no parent-figure or sibling smokes.

The attraction of Smoking for young people is its very inadmissibility. Most schools, and not a few homes - have clear Anti-Smoking Policies. Thus Smoking in school uniform◇ or on school grounds or behind neighbouring lock-up garages will probably be forbidden, punished◇ too. The same applies in the bedroom (?) the cafe or the youth club.

Another attraction is that Smoking is a very "adult" activity - whereas the children most tempted are not yet at that stage of their lives. Until recently, the packaging of cigarettes - in common with role models' Smoking - has been glamorous in the extreme. Also Smoking gets rid of many of the anxieties and frustrations that led to Truancy as an accompanying behaviour.

Truancy, by definition, allows far greater opportunity to Smoke ; more to obtain rations ; to trawl the gutters for discards; to share the same cigarette.

SNOW....3

Snow matters with Truancy because a clear double standard operates. The child who does not get to school because of Snow is told (s)he should have tried harder. After all, "most people managed the journey." On the other hand, if *the school* shuts because of Snow -

sometimes because of an inaccurate forecast of heavy snow - the child is told to go back home even *after* (s)he has successfully arrived for class. The question then arises: how deep does Snow need to be in the playground or on approach roads before closure? And does any amount of Snow prevent one big lesson for all-comers in the school hall?

SOCIAL CLASS....9

"Social Class" rather than "Class" is the more useful term when discussing Truancy: by definition absence from class! Social Class is *so* instrumental in Truancy that it is difficult to imagine Truancy divorced from Social Class.

It is almost as if Truancy cannot be disentangled from Social Class. Nobody can imagine the upper-class truant unless he is a privileged Little Lord Fauntleroy topped with straw hat nipping down the road from his public school to spend the proceeds of his postal order at the candy shop in town rather than swotting Latin Grammar in the study attached to his bedroom. Put another way, our view of Social Class is incomplete without the ghost of working-class habits past such as dossing, malingering, greyhound-racing, keeping coal in the bath, *Truancy* - and all the moral panic◇ surrounding such anti-social habits.

SOCIAL MEDIA....7

The Year 2004 witnessed the first year since the birth of Jesus when networking - indeed every type of social interaction - was possible without actually meeting another person in the flesh. Hitherto, a clumsy GPO landline, or a fax machine, or a receive-only pager, or a ring-back request, or a surface letter, pigeon, or battleground messenger had been the main means of keeping in touch with someone who might otherwise have disappeared from the radar screen.

Eventually, in a new Millennium, smart-phones reached out to *everyone*, *everywhere*, twenty-four hours a day. And, as with all good inventions, these unfamiliar Social Media brought problems: unjustified tracking◇, cyber-bullying◇, compulsive gambling, unlimited pornography, revenge postings, sleep deprivation, rudely interrupted holidays◇ and much more. Teenagers are *particularly* sensitive to adverse messaging, unflattering selfies, exclusion, also their wider popularity / unpopularity within the Facebook community.

SOCIAL RELATIONS....9

Not all children are equally equipped to face Social Relations / Social Relationships with enthusiasm. Some young people are fearfully shy, even to the extent of suffering school phobia◇. More commonly, gawky children feel they are inept in their Social Relations: a state of mind heavily reinforced by damning or demeaning messages on social media◇. And one response to this ineptitude is Truancy. After all, if one does not put oneself in the way of other people, there is no further need to worry (panic?) about how one will come across.

In the event of teachers recognizing that a child under their charge is acutely shy, a shrinking violet, petrified, awkward, isolated◇ or a rabbit in the headlamps, the first questions they need to ask each other is : "Has A/or B been sexually molested ?" or " Has A/ or B been witness to domestic violence ?" These are not pleasant suspicions, but are extremely relevant to most children in difficulty.

Conversely, there are a lot of means wise teachers can employ to reintegrate acutely bashful children. How about giving them a mentor◇? Or ascertaining whether (s)he is worried about bullying◇. Has a parent - maybe a single parent - got money worries? Then there is opportunity to give the marginalized◇ / ostracized child back into the frame: giving a little speech about fishing or knitting or classical music; drawing a cartoon for the notice-board; moving to a higher/ lower set◇. Any word of encouragement or praise◇, as opposed to criticism, counts. Also a discreet referral for home/school liaison◇ can help.

SPACING BETWEEN LESSONS....5

One remarkably simple device for easing the rush and tension of a typical school-day is to space lessons in an untraditional manner. Hardly any secondary school has ever allowed more than 3 or 4 minutes to get from one lesson to the next unless the school is split-site, or unless break or lunch-time intervenes.

Why not instead allow a minimum ten-minute gap between every single lesson or double period? Teachers would then arrive far less burdened or stressed; and pupils themselves would soon notice the difference and relax more. Another side-effect of wider spacing is the chance it affords for pupils to have a glass of water, to see somebody at the far end of campus, to change after Games or to ask for clarification of knowledge not understood.

SPORTING   BRILLIANCE....5

Sporting prowess / Sporting Brilliance both act as brakes on the dream of truanting. That is because Sport gives boys in particular a sense of purpose and validation◇ by the outside world. Also, *truants* might not be accepted in the team or for advance coaching. Another draw of the classroom is the chance to share footballing / snooker / rugby / cricket knowledge with equally knowledgeable - and disputatious - classmates.

STEP-PARENTHOOD
[SERIAL MONOGAMY]....7

It is the fate of half of all children that, at some point between the ages of 0 and 18, they will face fractured or altered parenthood. In other words, half of all children will not live those 18 years in the consistent charge of their birth mothers living with their birth fathers. A few will be fostered or adopted or taken into Care. Far more children, far more school pupils, will come home to find their new relatives are impromptu step-parents, serial monogamists, Mum's boyfriend, Dad's girlfriend, longer cohabitants, grandparents, strangers, whoever.

Most Step-Parents are very touchy when their commitment to children who are not their own offspring is brought into question, however obliquely. And many times, most days, and for most children, there is nothing to worry about. *Affected* school children can be far, far, more secure and well-maintained with Step-parents, surrogates or gay couples than with *birth fathers*◇ in particular: to the extent that amalgamated, reconstituted, families are becoming the norm rather than the exception.

All that accounted for, Step-children might not *see* their Step-father/ Step-mother as the best - even where the newly-harnessed birth parent is over the moon. Therefore, when the issue of school attendance arises, it is understandable that the suspected truant answers back: "Who are you...?" or "Lay off!" Tellingly, the very uncertainty surrounding Dad's choice of new girlfriend, Mum's choice of new boyfriend, might be inducement, or even reason, for the Truancy.

STEREOTYPING....9

Stereotyping is an enduring word-picture from the 1960s based on the invention of mimeograph, later the Xerox. Those doing the Stereotyping - which includes every single person - have a fixed image of what a yob or a tart or a "Paki" or a jihadi or a uni student or a parson or whoever will look like. "They're all the same!" Such lazy classifications involve mental short-cuts, attitudinal short-circuits.

Truants and those tempted◇ to truant are unlucky in that not only are they escaping◇ the stereotyping of others, less fortunate, at school and in their neighbourhoods ; not only do *they* pigeon-hole all the police, teachers and school- bobbies◇ they encounter in the course of their school evasion ; but also they themselves are heavily stereotyped because of their Truancy.

STIGMA....8

Stigma is Erving Goffman's expression of the insularity somebody might experience when marginalized◇ by the host society. So it is that the prisoner, the psychiatric patient, the drug addict◇, even the janitor is stigmatized. In fact, the host society *needs* Stigma in order to reinforce its own righteousness; its own superiority.

As folk-devil◇, the Truant has no exemption from being stigmatized. He is "other," not "one of us." He is escapee◇, and ignominious returnee◇, not attendee. He is fringe to other pupils' centrality. He it is who is not even entered for public examinations◇. Nor is he garlanded at the end-of-school Prom. And all the colloquialisms for Truancy: wagging, skiving, slacking, dossing, are pejorative enough to perpetuate Stigma.

SUICIDE / ATTEMPTED SUICIDE....8

Suicide is not uncommon among teenagers almost lost in the 6233 figure for all ages over 15, England and Wales, 2013. And it needs remembering: Suicide statistics are rendered speculative verging on useless because coroners bend over backwards to achieve open or accidental verdicts.

Also the public is obliged not to say $X+Y =$ the Z that is self-oblivion. Factors or predispositions will be raised at inquests, but rarely definitively. Should *school attendance* come up at an inquest or internal inquiry, it should be examined as part of whichever premature death is under scrutiny. Conversely, if school attendance is *not* raised, *it should be* - and then interrogated. A suicidal child might well have been feeling badly enough about self as imperative to truant first; then might have used an absence day to commit the act itself/ attempted act / just-in-time discovered act.

SUPERVISION ORDERS....7

A Supervision Order does not give the local authority parental responsibility for a child in need. However, it allows that authority to appoint a supervisor to advise, assist and befriend any supervised child; and to take whatever steps are necessary to make the Supervision Order work. Supervision Orders are normally made for six months or 12 months at time. They may be a good way of dealing with concerns which are worrying, but not serious enough for a Care Order. Supervision keeps an eye on the situation, monitoring progress/ regress.

Nor must the court opt for the weightier Care Order simply because that is what the local authority has requested. Ideally, courts value their independence.

SUMMER TERM....4

Summer Terms in Upper-School are a fluke. Not only is the weather a lot better and hotter than at other times in the year ; Summer Term traditionally contains the biggest block of examinations◊, mock examinations or public examinations. Not a few schools respond by *asking* 16- or 18-year olds not to come in at all unless it is for last-minute coaching or for the examinations themselves.

Authorized absence for revision◊, also authorized absence for recovery post-examination, does tend to happen more after May Day bank holiday than before. Nor any longer does *the majority* of head teachers encourage young people to *come back* to the classroom to help younger pupils with their reading / sports' day / private study ; nor necessarily does every head teacher insist that future A-level students return to their desks to get ready for 6th. Form challenges ahead.

SWIPE CARDS....10

In the past 40 years of chip-and-pin, we have witnessed the widespread introduction of both chips and bar-codes to access defined areas both on and off campus. In fact, Swipe Cards have come a long way in a relatively short time. The idea is that a door or gate or cubicle or classroom will only open by 32-hole + key-card configuration; sometimes infra-red ray as alternative.

However, all too many hotels, clubs, colleges and miners' welfares have learnt to their cost, and their aggravation, that Swipe Cards are never superior to the accompanying technology which in turn relies on human frailty. Then: what happens if the Swipe Card is lost, stolen or mislaid - or if it resides in another bag or item of clothing than the attendee has immediate access to ? In schools, locating or overriding the relevant Swipe Card might eat into the very lesson the forgetful child was due to attend in the first place!

TARGETS....8

Targets for Truancy are - at least on the surface - *nonsensical.* Because, in many ways - classically, with road casualty Targets - the goal should logically be set *at nought....* on the ground that any other figure would minimize the seriousness of any unfolding situation. So it is that many schools insist on *0%* failure to get an A-C in GCSE, *0%* noise in assembly, *0%* non-engagement in Community Service, Year 10, whatever.

Undaunted, a good number of local authorities still announce a new, verifiable *Attendance* Target of 92% - as opposed to 91% achieved in the previous year. And there is nothing to stop a solitary child being set an equally solitary Target : typically 85% of possible half-days in contrast with the 62 or 63% that has become his norm. That is when praise◇ is mandatory, once that new Target has been reached or surpassed. A similar Target might be set for homework◇, reprimands◇, or yellow cards - where football referee cards are issued for in-class misbehaviour◇.

TAUNTING....7

When children taunt each other, they are none too tactful or restrained. Some taunts come within the same bracket as tease/teasing - but it soon gets much more vicious than that: demeaning and degrading comments about a fellow-pupil's accent, background, dress◇, weight◇, make-up, sporting prowess◇, whatever. And those taunts can now conveniently be delivered by *remote control*: through the social media◇. Gang◇ taunts are horrible extensions of ordinary taunts.

Taunts would not be made if victims/survivors were neither sensitive nor susceptible to them. The fact that recipients are both sensitive *and* susceptible means terrible taunts are not mediated or set in context by better, kinder, truer, judgments. Therefore: at best the recipient stews; at worst she self-harms◇, stops eating◇, starts truanting, in order to escape◇ taunts.

TEMPTATION....8

The Temptation to bunk off School always increases with incentives: the possibility of *more* freedom, *more* pocket-money, *more* sport, *more* vouchers, *more* thrills.

The best way for a potential Truant to understand upcoming Temptation is to hold up the fingers of one hand before his or her face :- finger one: what *is* the Temptation? finger two : where is that Temptation coming from ? finger three : what would be the reward yielding to that Temptation ?   finger   four : what would be the repercussions, for good or ill, giving in to Temptation? finally, the thumb : *what happened last time I did, or did not do, that ?*

Some schools limit Temptation by having TVs in the classroom, letting boiled students have lessons outdoors, providing treats and reward points for good attendees, or by jazzing up - sexing up? - some of the more boring◇ lessons planned.

TOTALS TRUANTING....10

England and Wales' Totals Truanting, Scottish Totals also, are nigh impossible to calculate because of all the different categories of unauthorized absence, all the different categories *of authorized absence* from school.

A best guess - and it is only a post World War II *guess* - is that, at any one time 10% of pupils are not in the classroom, a fifth of this number (2% of all pupils) truanting. That's *before* regional, or cross-city, variations. In desultory snow, 100% of pupils play!

TRAVELLING   COMMUNITY [GYPSIES]....5

Romanies enjoy a very different way of life from the so-called *settled* community. Travellers may not *travel* every single day, or every single week, but their caravanning way of life is ill-adapted to fixed-site education. The same applies to the *Fairground* Community. Travelling children have very different needs and opportunities when compared with most of their peers◊. But do local authorities pick up that message before coming down heavy on Travellers for not promoting their children's classroom attendance?

A few local authorities have instituted quite specific Gypsy Outreach/ Gypsy Schools / Gypsies-in-School and Gypsy Self-Education programmes. Needless to say, Travellers are very suspicious of those same local authorities whose only perceived intent is to move them off-site to somewhere else. And formal Truancy proceedings, in Magistrates' Court◊, win no favours.

TRUANCY PATROLS....9

Truancy Patrols take many forms : EWOs◊ scouting round their patches, "Security" rooting out suspected truants from their shopping malls, vigilantes guarding their sheds and allotments, Police◊ making their trawl from local parks and chippies, head teachers themselves looking beyond their immediate school grounds, by driving round the estate in search of the lost!

Truancy Patrols are highly *controversial* - because truants are not criminals, nor should be defined as such; half-term holidays vary widely where local authority boundaries overlap ; ill◊ pupils might present as in good health on the surface; and there are the *additional* hazards of "offering" a lift back to school without putting the correct escorts◊ and permissions.

VARIABLE TERM TIMES
[VARIABLE SCHOOL YEARS] 6

For over 50 years there have been discussions surrounding Variable Term Times. Could there be 6 terms a year, not 3? Could Easter - a moveable feast - be *ignored* except for Good Friday and Easter Monday? Could *all* terms start January 1st., and end at Christmas? More exciting, could all boroughs / cities have random terms so that there would be less pressure on tourist destinations in Britain or abroad when school children are granted holiday from school at the same time? Are school and university terms needed *at all* ? They could each be replaced with one week off every 5 weeks.

Yet whenever counties / cities have *tried* to experiment, nothing much has worked. Here are a few of the experiments which have been tried, or proposed, already : Summer Holiday in late June / early July , to coincide with Wakes Week(s) ; beginning the Summer Term on or around April 16th. every single year; different university years from school years; the four-term year stretching from September year one to December year following ; *five* terms set at August 15th. to October 8th., October 22nd. to December 22nd.., January 8th. to March 1st.., March 15th. to April 30th., May 15th. to July 15th.; not to mention "Public School" terms, which have also been tried : three shortened, concentrated, terms of just 11 / 12 weeks each.

Opposition to *any change whatsoever* has arisen because : first, teachers tend to value *a long* Summer holiday ; second, teachers also value their 2 "religious" holidays : Christmas and Easter ; third, many parents and teachers and sibling groups◇ straddle local education authority areas ; fourth, September 1st. has "always" been the start of the year ; fifth, public examinations◇ happen every May and June - and appear to be non-negotiable ; sixth, the existing structure underlines the "truth" that most of 12 month's school-work gets done before Christmas ; also seventh, existing terms tend to accommodate the weather.

Term times impact upon *Truancy* in these ways : dreadful weather, if it comes, comes in peak school time January 3rd. to March 25th.; some very *hot* weather occasionally comes within traditional school term time as well : June 7th to July 20th.; truants are not entered into as many public examinations◇ as are 100% attendees ; the Autumn Term in particular seems everso formidable; and the piecemeal, happenstance, system of the present makes Truancy almost impossible to detect by Police◇ and shopkeepers *for at least a week* before and after every school holiday, including before and after half-term holidays.

VICTIMIZATION / VICTIMHOOD 8

Mirroring a parent's possible Victimization at work and in the street, an *unusual* child, perhaps the child of travellers◇ or incomers, also assumes Victimhood. And because Victimhood is a notoriously wobbly jelly, one grievance or imagined slight tends to build upon another till the whole edifice collapses. The word *"Survivor"* is a better word than "Victim" - and far more *constructive* - which is the reason the "disabled" Child should correctly be called the differently-abled. child.

Victimhood does however carry within its orbit the advantage that it is the perfect excuse for persistent absence from the classroom. Should any teacher attempt to assert *the opposite*, a child is quite within her rights to reply: "Can't you *see* the colour of my skin? / state of my shoes? / moved-on caravan? / self-harming scars? / or Facebook account laden with hatred ?

Very many Truants have, sadly, never been able to see themselves as *other than* Victims. They cannot thank God for small mercies because they have yet to experience *any* mercy, any blessing. And, right into the midst of this Victimhood, in will step the courts seen as equally insensitive to everyone else.

WAGGING....by definition   **See Bunking Off**

[THE] WEATHER

Good Weather can result in a spike in the number of truants. Equally, *Bad* Weather can result in a spike in the number of Truants. Weather is everso influential in all our journey plans. Economically deprived pupils find both hot and cold weather a challenge. Have I the right footwear? New tee-shirt required? An anorak for protection? An umbrella for shelter? School bus◊ - or ordinary bus? And will I be able to concentrate?

Schools might do better to revive Horticulture, Nature Studies, Social Opinion / traffic movement surveys: as possible alternatives to classroom-bound lessons. Where more pupils are absent on one particular freezing

Monday or one particular roasting Friday, a link with the Weather is surprisingly easy to establish and to work on.

WILL MUM STILL BE THERE ?....6

Hundreds of pupils attempt Truancy every single day because they fear that what has happened to Mum - maybe *Dad*, if he is the single parent - may lead her to walk out forever. In repeat instances of marital rape, mental and physical cruelty, it would be unsurprising if the loyalest of Mums was *not* ready to walk out and not come back.

Thus an equally loyal son or daughter stays at home to "protect" Mum; to keep an eye on her; maybe to provide a flimsy shield for her when a grown man's wrath spills over. Yet there is no category of *authorized* absence from school: *Keeping the Family Together*.

WITHDRAWAL FROM CLASS [FROM SCHOOL] 8

Many, if not most, Withdrawals of Child from Class are symbolic of an irretrievable breakdown of trust◊ between aggrieved parent/guardian and exasperated place of learning. Withdrawal of a child might follow bullying◊, detention◊, religious education, sex education◇, sexual molestation on school premises, "victimization"◇, school uniform◇ restrictions, haircuts - or the imposition of a Penalty Notice.

In an ideal world, a child would be withdrawn on a Friday afternoon and be taken into a different academy the following Monday, 11am. But such easy transitions *just do not happen*. What follows Withdrawal is lengthy correspondence, also escalated animosity, between parent-figure and local education authority. And such stand-offs have a lot in common with Truancy as protest.

WORLD CUP....4

The World Cup is included here as a totemic event; the pinnacle of perceived sporting prowess◇; just the sort of attraction likely to appear more attractive than school lessons.

Men, in particular, are known to have a highly transferrable interest in what's on telly. If it's not the World Cup, it's the UEFA Cup. If it's not the Six Nations', it's the Benson and Hedges. If it's not the Olympics, it's snooker from the Crucible. And that sustains our image of the couch potato as the man slumped in his armchair with a fag in his mouth, a Fosters' six-pack perched on the arm-rest.

Some sports strive to put on their highlights outside of school hours. But that is not always possible. Just as Personnel Officers have no difficulty matching staff absences with Mondays, Fridays, the Derby and Aintree, so School Attendance Officers◇ have no difficulty spotting a parade nearby, a heat wave or the World Cup qualifying rounds.

WORN OUT....6

Truants themselves are more likely to be Worn Out than the rest of the school population, due to extra caring responsibilities◇; unauthorized earning opportunities◇; participation in the night economy; sleeplessness◇ ; poverty◇ ; sibling rivalry◇; also the sheer degree of energy consumed evading detection◇. And if the Truant *is* Worn Out, that leads to a deterioration in future attendance.

WORTHLESSNESS....7

The outsider is often absolutely baffled that anybody, particularly a pleasant, maybe good-looking, teenager with the whole world ahead of him or her should feel totally worthless. What messages must that child have received from birth that (s)he shouldn't have been born, and, once born, shouldn't have been trouble 24/7 ?

Worthlessness matters in the debate on Truancy: as so many school evaders do actually feel valueless, no use to man or beast. This puts scoring yourself low, lower, lowest, in the same bracket as the eating disorder◇, self-harm◇....at worst, suicide◇.

YOUTH CLUBS....5

Youth Clubs had their heyday in the 1960s, 70s and 80s, coinciding with a revival in the Youth Hostel Association, also Outward Bound. But Youth Clubs turned out to be the lowest hanging fruits when local authorities were faced with austerity, and the need to make cuts. Very, very few detached youth workers are now being trained or offered relevant job opportunities.

The Youth Club, fundamentally, is the perfect answer to children put out on the streets. In Liverpool, post Toxteth, what the Club could offer was famously called "ping-pong therapy." Clubs used to take Mods as well as Rockers, non-conformists as well as conformists, litter-droppers as well as litter-pickers. Many adolescents looked forward to Youth Club night. No

longer. Yet their closure is probably short-sighted penny-pinching, parsimony disregarding pundits who want youngsters "off the street"
.

YOUTH COURT [S] 7

Youth Courts, by definition, only see, or punish◇, or put forward for trial *troubled* children: yet not so troubled as to have committed murder, manslaughter, GBH or rape. So Youth Courts also see hundreds of truants each year, but *not* to address their Truancy.

The youth magistrate's art is to disentangle ABH, criminal damage, shop theft or riding a moped without lights from unauthorized absence from the classroom. Weight here must be given to the offence rather than the offender - except, perhaps, where the offence was actually committed *on a truanting day.*

YOUTH UNEMPLOYMENT....10

The importance of Youth Unemployment in the Truancy debate is impossible to underestimate or to overestimate. Youth Unemployment spreads its tentacles everywhere : not least to those qualified, and unqualified, young adults who want to work, don't want to work, want to earn, want - or not want - to learn whilst earning ; affecting everyone else in society.

Youth Unemployment: variously estimated at *between 1 and 2 million* young people out of work, eliminated from employment, in a way, *forbidden* employment, overlooked for employment, perhaps *priced out* of employment, lacking the skills for employment, unready for employment.

So it is nobody speaks or writes about Youth Unemployment without referring to *"wastage"* or "being thrown on the scrap-heap." Easy it is point the finger of blame at somebody, or some group, for high, higher, stratospheric, Youth Unemployment : the Government, obviously ; small and medium enterprises not taking on apprentices◇ ; older workers not retiring ; shopkeepers looking to go self-service ; robots; interactive computer technology ; minimum wage legislation ; teachers for not teaching enough ; universities turning out too many or too few graduates ; smog, whatever. But principally it is the young adult himself - normally a he - or the young girl prematurely pregnant◇, or the ex-truant, or the early drug addict◇, or the late riser◇, or the "dosser," blamed for their own Unemployment.

The truth is: some corporate targets are too valued, too powerful, too remote, ever to be criticized, so making it more practical *to blame the victim*. If a Corporation meets in New York and decides to axe its British operation ; if a chain suddenly shuts 430 of its stores ; if a bank decides to downsize ; or if a call centre relocates overseas with some its biggest clients outsourcing their manufacturing overseas, these are targets too big, too precious, too iconic, to criticize for their inestimable impact on Youth Unemployment - and sometimes middle-aged Unemployment - leaving young adults themselves "responsible" for their idleness.

Very soon, despairing teenagers are also blamed - and threatened with *benefit sanctions* - for not writing enough CVs; not sending in enough application forms; not putting in for enough job interviews; not being flexible enough in their ambitions; not achieving high enough grades in exams; not getting up early enough in the morning ; famously, *not getting on their bikes* ; not caring about the financially stretched parents they still live with ; and not turning up enough at Job Centre.

Teenagers out of work in Redcar are censured just as much as Londoners. Teenagers out of work in the South Wales Valleys are censured as much of those residing in Britain's Silicone Valleys, the land of milk and honey. Black teenagers at a loose end are judged just as harshly as white teenagers. Also teenagers totally abandoned by their families, step families◇ and adoptive families are judged as unsympathetically as Unemployed teenagers from close, loving and supportive households. Plenty of concentration on micro casualties; no investigation at all of macro-economics

Now the truant or intending truant only has to observe a "sink school"; only has to live in a 1970s Council Estate where joblessness is a way of life; only has to read the local newspaper on closures and redundancies; only has to pass a once-proud boarded up factory, to decide that formal education is little use if it only qualifies you to be disqualified from the opportunities freely available to foregoing generations.

ΩΨΩΨΩΨΩΨΩΨΩΨΩΨΩΨΩ

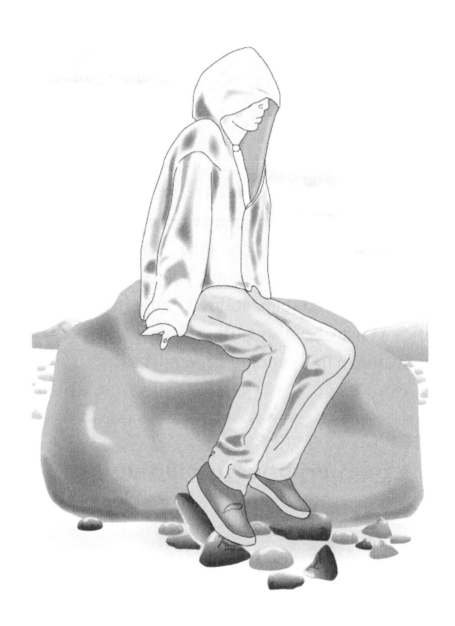

DE-BRIEFING THE TRUANT :
POSSIBLE AVENUES

....

*** tell me a bit more about your day away

*** you must have been very fearful of discovery ?

*** money must be a real problem for you

*** your phone looks ancient !

*** it doesn't appear your alarm-clock's much use ?

*** I'm lost how you balance all those demands
people are making on you....

*** there might be grants for books and uniform

*** I don't think I could survive on top of a double-decker

*** *Facebook* has really got to you

*** maybe your parents, too,
were worried where you'd got to?

*** *that* particular lesson we might take another look at

*** just look at this string of A's in the Register !

*** it struck me your weight-loss [weight-gain] has
troubled you a lot more of late ?

ADDRESSING TRUANCY : A TEN-POINT PLAN

....

1) Each school to have a Truancy ground-plan;

2) Each school to have - or to share - a part-time
Truant & Truancy Research Officer;

3) Each Academy, Free School or LEA to devise a
Non-Punitive Truancy Response Strategy;

4) Pupil Poverty to be uppermost in any Response -
even if it turns out to be a red herring;

5) The possibility of Domestic Violence to be
considered in each and every Truancy Response;

6) The possibility of familial / or stranger Sexual Abuse
to be considered in each and every Truancy Response;

7) The actual / suspected truant to be taken up /
or taken in as a whole person, not just an absentee;

8) Each school / EWO to work on
an everyday Locality Profile;

9) Each suspected truant to have a Family Tree;

10) Every "hostile" parent to be treated as an ally.

ΩΨΩΨΩΨΩΨΩΨΩΨΩΨΩ

T R U A N C Y :

A SELECT BIBLIOGRAPHY

[arranged by title, alphabetically]

....

Adolescence [*John W. Santrock*] 2009

Adolescence :Aspects of Modern Society
[*Cyril S. Smith*] 1968

ASBO Nation: The Criminalisation of Nuisance
[*ed. Peter Squires*] 2008

The Attendance Toolkit: Practical Activities for
Addressing Absence in Young People Aged 6-13
[*Catherine Roberts*] 2015

Behaviour for Learning: Proactive Approaches to
Behaviour Management [*Simon Ellis & Janet Tod*]
2009

Behaviour in Schools Paperback
[*Louise Porter*] 2006

Boys, Girls and Achievement: Addressing the
Classroom Issues [*Becky Francis*] 2000

contd....

Bullying at School: What We Know and What We Can Do .....Understanding Children's Worlds
[*Dan Olweus*] 1993

Bullying: Effective Strategies for Long-term Change .....School Concerns Series
[*Tiny Arora & Sonia Sharp*] 2002

Bullying in Schools [*ed. Delwyn P. Tattum*] 1989

Deschooling Society [*Ivan Illich*] 1971

The Dictionary of Feminist Theory
[*Maggie Humm*] 2003

Don't Fence Me In: Essays on the Rational Truant: The Empty Desk Syndrome
[*ed. Michael Conolly & Dennis O'Keeffe*]   2009

An Essential Guide to Improving Attendance in your School..... Practical resources for all school managers [*Ken Reid*] 2013

Feeling Like Crap: Young People and the Meaning of Self-Esteem [*Nick Luxmoore*] 2008

5 Quick and Easy Solutions to Common Classroom Disruptions
[*Bryan Harris and Cassandra Goldberg*] 2012

Fixing Truancy Now: Inviting Students Back to Class [*Jonathan Shute & Bruce S. Cooper*] 2014

Generation X
[*Charles Hamblett & Jane Deverson*] 1964

Generation Z: Their Voices, Their Lives
[*Chloe Combi*] 2015

Growing Out of Crime: Society and Young People in Trouble [*Andrew Rutherford*] 1986

Helping Teenagers with Anger & Low Self-Esteem
[*Ed. Margot Sunderland*] 2012

How to Stop Bullying in Classrooms and Schools: Using Social Architecture to Prevent, Lessen, and End Bullying [*Phyllis Kaufman Goodstein*] 2013

How to Talk So Teens Will Listen and Listen So Teens Will Talk
[*Adele Faber & Elaine Mazlish*] 2006

Improving Behaviour and Attendence at School
[*Susan Hallam & Lynne Rogers*] 2008

Just Ticking the Box?: Refocusing School Attendance [*Ben Whitney*] 2014

contd....

Managing School Attendance: Successful
Intervention Strategies for Reducing Truancy
[*Ken Reid*] 2013

The Passage from Boyhood to Manhood: Seven
Truths Fathers Need to Tell Their Sons
[*David R. Grimm*] 2010

Pupils Absence and Truancy from Schools in
England 2000/2001 Bulletin [*DfE*] 2002

Report on Juvenile Delinquency
[*Mass Observation*] 2009

Ringleaders and Sidekicks: How to Help Your Son
Cope with Classroom Politics, Bullying, Girls and
Growing Up [*Rosalind Wiseman*] 2013

School Counsellors Working with Young People and
Staff: A Whole-School Approach
[*Nick Luxmoore*] 2013

Schooling the Smash Street Kids....Crisis Point
[*Paul Corrigan*] 1979

Schools Out: Truancy and Exclusion
[*Emilie Goodall*] 2005

contd...

The Step-Parents' Parachute: The Four Cornerstones of Good Step-Parenthood [*Flora McEvedy*] 2009

Tackling Teenage Pregnancy: Sex, Culture and Needs [*Ruth Chambers et al.*] 2000

Teenage Brain [*Frances E. Jelsen*] 2015

Truancy and Social Welfare: Bells Ringing in the Distance [*Godfrey Holmes*] 1989

The Truancy Myth [*Ben Whitney*] 2011

Truancy Prevention and Intervention: A Practical Guide [*Lynne Bye et al.*] 2010

Truancy Revisited: Students as School Consumers [*Rita Guare & Bruce S. Cooper*] 2003

Truancy, School Exclusion and Substance Misuse [*Lesley McAra*] 2004

Truancy: Short and Long-term Solutions: Working with Teachers, Pupils and Schools [*Ken Reid*] 2002

Truancy: The Politics of Compulsory Schooling [*Pat Carlen*] 1992

contd....

Understanding and Dealing with Cyberbullying: A guide for Teachers [*Dawn Hewitson et al.*] 2016

Working with Anger and Young People [*Nick Luxmoore*] 2006

Working with Young People [*Ed. Sheila Curran*] 2013

Young Offenders [*Frank Pakenham*] 1993

Young Offenders and the Law: How the Law Responds to Youth Offending [*Raymond Arthur*] 2010

Your Conversation - or Mine ? 200 Tactics When Talking [*Godfrey Holmes*] 1999

ΩΨΩΨΩΨΩΨΩΨΩΨΩΨΩ

The Author will be really pleased to hear of new entries to this Dictionary by chance not included already companion to this volume :

....

A DICTIONARY OF

OPPRESSION IN

THE WORKPLACE

by: Godfrey Holmes

Nethermoor Books

March 2015

ISBN : 978-0-953-6016-5-3

an   invaluable guide to
relations at work - and
a first ever comprehensive A to Z

Lightning Source UK Ltd.
Milton Keynes UK
UKOW07f0359250715

255813UK00004B/58/P